MW01074037

THE
SAMURAI
MIND

myou   mysterious

THE SAMURAI MIND

Lessons from Japan's Master Warriors

CHRISTOPHER HELLMAN

TUTTLE Publishing
Tokyo | Rutland, Vermont | Singapore

Published by Tuttle Publishing, an imprint of Periplus Editions (HK) Ltd.

www.tuttlepublishing.com

Copyright © 2010 Christopher Hellman

Library of Congress Cataloging-in-Publication Data

Hellman, Christopher.
 The samurai mind : lessons from Japan's master warriors / Christopher Hellman.
   p. cm.
 ISBN 978-0-8048-4115-3 (hardcover)
1. Swordplay--Japan. 2. Samurai. 3. Martial arts--Japan. I. Title.
 GV1150.H45 2010
 796.860952--dc22

                          2010023987

ISBN 978-0-8048-4115-3
ISBN 978-4-8053-1155-4 (For sale in Japan only)

Distributed by

North America, Latin America & Europe
Tuttle Publishing
364 Innovation Drive
North Clarendon, VT 05759-9436 U.S.A.
Tel: 1 (802) 773-8930
Fax: 1 (802) 773-6993
info@tuttlepublishing.com
www.tuttlepublishing.com

Asia Pacific
Berkeley Books Pte. Ltd.
61 Tai Seng Avenue #02-12
Singapore 534167
Tel: (65) 6280-1330
Fax: (65) 6280-6290
inquiries@periplus.com.sg
www.periplus.com

Japan
Tuttle Publishing
Yaekari Building, 3rd Floor
5-4-12 Osaki Shinagawa-ku
Tokyo 141 0032
Tel: (81) 3 5437-0171
Fax: (81) 3 5437-0755
www.tuttle.co.jp

First edition
12 11 10 09 08   10 9 8 7 6 5 4 3 2 1

Printed in Singapore

Contents

Introduction 7

The Mysterious Skills of the Old Cat 17

Sword Theory 25

A Treatise on the Sword 31

Joseishi's Discussions on the Sword 46

Ignorance in Swordsmanship 100

Acknowledgments 127

Introduction

The sword occupies a central position in the martial culture and history of Japan. It is surrounded by layers of mystique, extending from its forging through to almost every aspect of its care and use. Above all it is associated with the samurai, the hereditary military class that rose to ascendance towards the end of the 12th century, and continued to hold power until the social upheavals that resulted in the birth of "modern" Japan in the 1860s.

It holds this position despite the fact that in more than three centuries of warfare, until Tokugawa Ieyasu's victory at the Battle of Sekigahara (1603), which ushered in a period of over two hundred and fifty years of relative peace, the principal weapon of the samurai on the battlefield had never been the sword. Originally evolving as mounted archers, their primary weapon, the bow, was superseded by the spear as the weapon of choice during the aptly named *Sengoku* period—The Age of The Country at War. But the sword had always been with the samurai; from the time of their emergence as a distinct class they had carried swords, and the importance which was attached to them can be gauged by the fact that as early as the 10th century CE important blades were known by name. Throughout this period of warfare, great care and attention was put into the making of swords—Masamune, regarded as perhaps the greatest swordsmith in Japanese history, was working in the late 13th and early 14th centuries, and even during the bloody years of the *Sengoku* period important blades were highly valued, being passed down as heir-looms or presented as marks of great distinction. It is clear that swords were regarded as something more than simply tools of warfare.

The year 1603 saw the beginning of a new era in Japanese history: the unification of the country under the military government of the Tokugawa family, a time of peace. After some hundred and fifty years of continuous warfare, the warrior class found the skills it had specialized in on the verge of redundancy. At first the samurai maintained their primarily military role, but by the late 17th century it was clear that many other areas of duty, chiefly in the bureaucratic field, superseded the need for skill at arms. Despite the changes they experienced, the samurai retained their position as a warrior class, an identity that had been reinforced by the tightening of strictures on class and social mobility. While many samurai were fully absorbed in their non-military roles, significant numbers continued to preserve and develop the skills they had inherited from previous generations. For most, this meant the art of swordsmanship.

Without the threat of imminent warfare, the style of weapon use taught by the various schools of martial arts evolved with the changing lifestyle of the samurai. Weapons such as the spear were sidelined and techniques developed for use in armor were replaced by those capitalizing on the increased mobility afforded by everyday wear. Indeed, since the sword itself was worn on a daily basis by the samurai, it was during this time that it assumed an unchallenged position as foremost amongst the weapons of the samurai, and swordsmanship became their principal martial art. The sword also became the focus of the samurai's martial identity and much energy was put into the search for perfection in swordsmanship, with a proliferation of styles and approaches. In this period of peace, the considerations that went into training were understandably different from those of the pre-Tokugawa period; although the newer styles had become increasingly refined and subtle and it was not long before questions arose as to their effectiveness, and without the opportunity to test them in battle, the value of the older training methods was also called into question. In a move to reinstate combative efficiency, the use of flexible bamboo swords and protective training equipment was introduced in some schools, allowing a form of sparring. These innovations were instrumental in the eventual development of what is now known as kendo, a discipline in which the aim is not to develop skills with the sword as a means of combat, but as a vehicle for personal growth.

In truth, however, even before the Tokugawa Period, the study of swordsmanship held an important, even primary place, in the teaching of many of the schools of martial arts. These schools or styles, the martial ryu, were the means of preserving and transmitting the martial arts. They were mainly embodied in lineages of teachers who passed down the arts from generation to generation. The number of schools ran into the hundreds, some of which are still practiced in some form to this day. Some of them specialized in a single weapon, while others included a range of weaponry in their curriculum. Other military schools were not concerned directly with the use of weapons at all, but taught skills such as horsemanship, strategy, or swimming while encumbered with armor. Those schools that did include swordsmanship in their teachings seem to have accorded it a very important place in their styles. Though many of these styles date from some four hundred years ago or more, as far as we can tell from the traditions passed down to us today, the sword served not only as an introduction to the techniques of these styles, but also as an embodiment of many of the most important principles of the style.

The basic teachings of many of the individual schools most

likely had much in common, but the more advanced techniques were shrouded in secrecy. A major part of these teachings were passed down in the form of kata—pre-arranged patterns in the form of short combative exchanges, usually between two partners, which served to teach not only important aspects of weapons use such as the understanding of rhythm and timing, judgment of distance and preferred target areas, but also embodied deeper principles of combat. As the students continued in their practice, internalizing these aspects, they would learn increasingly difficult kata, which allowed them to apply the techniques with greater ease and effectiveness. A sharp line was drawn between the basic techniques of the ryu, which were deemed adequate for normal trainees, and the more advanced levels. Admittance to these higher levels of instruction required proof of dedication and loyalty as well as proven ability acquired through long years of hard training. Upon achieving a full understanding of the higher levels of technique, the student would sometimes set up their own branch school, often differentiating it from their teacher's school by slightly altering the name. Alternatively, they might continue in their quest for martial skills by searching for other teachers, or undergoing periods of intense, solitary training. If they felt they had achieved an understanding significantly different from that of their teacher, they might give their school a completely new name.

Successful completion of advanced levels of training would usually result in the granting of some kind of certification from the master of the school. Often this would be in the form of a list of techniques that would mean very little to an outsider. Even more discursive documents such as the well known *Go Rin No Sho* of Miyamoto Musashi or the various writings of the Yagyu Family were originally handwritten documents intended for very limited circulation, to be seen only by those who were already familiar with the details of the techniques and concepts to which they referred. Often their terse descriptions of techniques end with such admonitions as "You must study this hard." In this sense they were not meant to describe, but served as reinforcement or spurs for further study, as well as proofs of legitimacy of a line of teaching.

The texts presented in this selection are very different. They were written from the mid-18th to the early 19th century, at precisely the time when the effectiveness of the methods of training in swordsmanship were being called into question; more significantly, they were written for a wider audience than just the masters' own inner coterie of advanced students—possibly some were intended for beginning or intermediate students but others were clearly meant for complete outsiders. Their aim was to explain their respective arts, and they do so with great insight. What is common to all of them is their focus on the essence of the art as something that cuts across styles. They take a critical stance towards the view of swordsmanship simply as a collection of physical techniques, emphasizing the importance of the development of inner factors involving the mind and the spirit: it was this, rather than the skilled physical manipulation of the blade, that was responsible for the incredible abilities of the sword masters of old.

This aspect of swordsmanship appears to have been part of the schools of martial arts since their beginnings, with the resulting abilities often attributed to divine inspiration. Many of the early schools maintained close links to shrines and sacred sites, and their practitioners undertook extended periods of ascetic training with the aim of achieving a kind of martial enlightenment. Explicit references may be found in many of the extant documents of schools from the 15th century onwards, as well as in preserved oral traditions, and even in the very names of some of the schools. Zen Buddhism, appears to have been less influential than is commonly imagined, playing a rather minor role in martial schools as a whole. Individual practitioners seem to have held a variety of religious affiliations, but these did not necessarily reflect or influence the teachings of traditional schools. In each of the texts presented here, any references to religion occur merely as part of the cultural milieu, and indeed, during this period the dominant philosophical school of thought was not religious but secular: Neo-Confucianism.

Chinese thought and culture had long been respected and admired in Japan, and over the centuries there had been a steady, if irregular, import of ideas from the Asian mainland. The establishment of Tokugawa power coincided with the spread of teaching of the Neo-Confucian schools that had developed in the Song Dynasty. The Tokugawas were quick to promote these teachings, ensuring their widespread influence. Although it has tended to be associated almost wholly with the moral and ethical education of the samurai class and the consequent maintenance of hierarchical relationships in society, the texts in this selection illustrate how Confucian references were also used to explain theoretical aspects of swordsmanship that are often assumed to be the sole province of Zen. In fact, it can be seen that masters drew from a variety of sources, often irrespective of their origin, to explain their arts. Despite occasional differences in terminology, the concepts that are discussed are remarkably similar. Above all, the writers of the texts in this selection were men of their times, and their writing is firmly situated in the culture of their day, and a background (in the case of all but one of them) of personal mastery in the arts they describe. True to their experience, they stress that though the higher aspects of swordsmanship are mysterious, they are the result of martial, not spiritual, training.

The works presented here, spanning almost exactly a hundred years, from the early 18th to 19th centuries, have much in common, though each echoes the distinctive voice of the author.

The Mysterious Skills of the Old Cat (*Neko no Myojutsu*) (1727) is the only one of these works that was not written by a master swordsman, but paradoxically it provides an excellent key to understanding the essence of this art. It is, of course, a story, but a delightful one which outlines different approaches or levels of attainment in the practice of martial arts through the attitudes of different cats which are brought in to rid a samurai's house of a ferocious rat. Although it works on the surface level as a parable, its depiction of the inner factors involved in swordsmanship is surprisingly accurate. A close reading of the story shows correspondences to the other texts on significant points, reinforcing the supposition that Chozan was, indeed, knowledgeable on matters of the sword, even if he was not a master himself.

Sword Theory (*Kensetsu*) (1789-1803) and *A Treatise on the Sword* (*Kencho*) (1804), were both written by Hirayama Shiryu. In the first, Hirayama presents his uncompromising theory on the use of the sword. Straightforward and direct, this illustrates the quintessential samurai spirit. Hirayama was also a man of some considerable learning and, evidently, a sense of self-deprecating humor, rounding off the work with "A Verse of Eight Follies." As the reader will soon realize, the subject of this verse is the author himself. In *A Treatise on the Sword*, he develops his theory by offering examples drawn from classical Chinese works to give it more authority and weight. For his readership, this was a sort of "proof" that Hirayama wasn't simply expressing his personal opinions. Although written when Hirayama was in his early forties, it is thought the later date on the preface of *Sword Theory* may refer to the addition of "A Verse of Eight Follies" and the combination with *A Treatise on the Sword*. Although originally intended for a select audience, they are very different in tone from the "secret" works of earlier generations. The two were published together for a wider audience in 1870.

In a similar way, *Joseishi's Discussions on the Sword* (*Joseishi Kendan*) (1810) also draws heavily on classical sources; in fact it draws upon a whole range of sources from Noh plays to medical books. Although attribution is not certain, the work is generally considered to have been written by Matsuura Shozan, a literary figure as well as a swordsman, (the Joseishi of the title) who was well known for a collection of essays in the form of an extended travel diary. This approach is reflected in this work: it is a selection of seemingly random observations and advice on aspects of swordsmanship which build up to give us an intriguing personal view of this warlike art in a time of peace. At times pithy, at others prolix, he takes considerable pains to explain what may seem quite minor points, while disposing of more practical matters in a few sentences. Again and again, Matsuura returns to similar themes, showing how swordsmanship relates to daily life, to the role of a samurai, and how seemingly minor details and attitudes are the first steps to learning the secrets of the art.

Ignorance in Swordsmanship (*Fushikihen*) (1764) is the most theoretical of the works. It is easy to regard this kind of writing as "mere" theorizing, especially as it includes something of a moral element, and some commentators have chosen to treat it as a work of philosophy, rather than explore its practical dimensions. However the traditional martial arts deal with concepts that are, by their very nature, difficult to explain precisely in words, though being no less concrete for all that. The style that the author writes about has its origins in the use of the spear—perhaps the most uncompromisingly practical hand-to-hand weapon in the samurai arsenal. Despite the philosophical tone of his writing, realism is at the very heart of his approach to achieving mastery in the use of the sword.

The Writers

Issai Chozan (1659–1741) was the pen name of Niwa Juro-zaemon Tadaaki. Relatively little is known about him, but he was a prolific writer known for his collection of stories, *Inaka Soji* (1727) (*Rustic Zhuangzi*), in which *The Mysterious Skills of the Old Cat* originally appeared. Though avowedly not a master of the sword himself, it is thought he pursued studies in the martial as well as literary arts, and both *The Mysterious Skills of the Old Cat* and his other work on swordsmanship *Tengu Geijitsuron* have been included in anthologies of martial arts writing since the 18th century.

Hirayama Shiryu (1759–1828) was born into a military family; although he was educated in the government college and well versed in a variety of academic areas, he threw the full weight of his enthusiasm into the martial arts, studying a variety of styles and different weapons, including the use of firearms and horsemanship. He named his school the Chuko-Shinkan-ryu. He lived an austere life, practicing hundreds of thrusts and cuts on a daily basis. A contemporary describes his practice hall as filled with spears, *naginata*, wooden swords, muskets, suits of armor, and even three cannon. He also wrote several hundred works on a variety of subjects of which the two presented here are probably the best known.

Matsuura Kiyoshi Seizan (Joseishi)(1760–1841) became Lord of the domain of Hirado at the age of fifteen. After some years, the clan headship was transferred to his younger brother in 1806. Following this enforced retirement he took up writing, making a name as a literary figure, but continued to devote himself to the study of the Shingyoto-ryu style of swordsmanship. He was recognized as a 6th generation master of the style in 1786, and was given the name Joseishi. He wrote several other works on swordsmanship, but his rank ensured he had no need to teach professionally. Even late in life his skills were still impressive: he was recorded as having decisively won a "friendly" contest at the age of 77.

Kimura Kyuhou (c.1704–1764) is little is known beyond the few details he gives in the works he published. He also wrote *Unchu-ryu Kenjutsu Youryou* (*Essentials of Unchu-ryu Swordsmanship*) which he published together with the *Honshiki Sanmondou* of Kimura Sukekurou Tomoshige (1580-1656) a student of the Yagyu Shinkage-ryu. (Interestingly, Hirayama Shiryu practiced a style of Unchu-ryu founded by Kimura Sukekurou Tomoshige, becoming the 4th headmaster.) Kimura Kyushou's Unchu-ryu swordsmanship seems closely connected to the Yagyu Shinkage-ryu, and it seems likely that the sword skills added to the school by his teacher came directly from that school. He was named by his teacher as the second generation successor of the Echizen Unchu-ryu.

The Mysterious Skills
Of The Old Cat
(Neko No Myoujutsu)

Issai Chozan

Once there was a swordsman called Shoken. A large rat had
appeared in his house one day and started running about even
though it was broad daylight. He shut it up in a room and set
his cat to catch it. As the cat crept forward, the rat leapt at her
face and bit her. The cat yowled and bolted out of the room.

After this setback, Shoken rounded up a group of cats
from the neighborhood who were known as good mousers,
and herded them into the room. There was the rat, sitting in
the corner. When one of them approached, the rat sprang forward and bit it. Faced with that horrible sight, the other cats
drew back and refused to tackle it again.

Shoken was so angry he picked up a wooden sword, in-
tending to kill the rat himself. He chased it around, but it
dodged so well he couldn't hit it—instead the paper doors and
screens around the walls were reduced to tatters. Fast as lightning it leapt in the air straight for his face. Shoken felt sure he
was going to get bitten.

Dripping with sweat, he called his servant. "A little way
from here," he said, "there's a really marvelous cat I've heard
about. I want you to go and find it, and bring it back here."

But when he saw the cat the servant brought back, he wasn't impressed. It didn't look tough or clever or particularly fast. Still, he opened the door a little, and let the cat into the room to see what it could do. When it entered, the rat sat motionless. The cat did nothing, just walked slowly over, grabbed the rat, and brought it out in his mouth.

That evening, the cats gathered in Shoken's house, and requesting that the old cat take the place of honor, knelt down before him. "We have all trained hard and are well known for hunting rats as well as other animals like otters and weasels. Our claws are always kept sharp, but we have never experienced anything like the power of that rat. But with your technique, you easily subdued it. Please teach us all you can of your mysterious art," they asked with great respect.

The old cat laughed and said, "You young cats have certainly worked quite hard, but because you've never been taught the true approach you were defeated when you ran into a situation outside your experience. Before we go any further, lets hear about the kind of training you had."

A smart looking black cat came forward. "I was born into a family of rat catchers and have trained hard in the art since I was a kitten. I can jump over tall screens, wriggle through small holes, and perform all manner of acrobatics. I can feign sleep and be awake in an instant when rats come to pester me. Even scampering across beams and pillars, they're not safe from me. But that rat today was so much stronger than I had thought—all my training seemed wasted. I wouldn't have believed it."

The old cat replied, "What you have learned is only outward form and techniques. That's why you were unsuccessful. Outer forms are taught to indicate the direction we should follow, so though they do, in fact, contain the truth—but if you specialize in them, jumping from one to another and devising new variations, you will lack the essence of the skills of the old masters. Using your own cleverness, you'll end up as a collector of techniques and your skill will amount to nothing. The height of skill of common people, of all those who rely on cleverness, is like this. Though cleverness involves the mind, it is not based on the true path. To concentrate only on skill is limiting and, in fact, your reliance on cleverness can lead to much harm. Take this advice, reflect, and carefully reconsider your progress."

Next, a large striped cat stepped forward. "In my opinion, the use of energy is what is most important in fighting, and so I have been training my *ki* for many years. Now it is so powerful, it reaches to the skies. I can have the enemy at my feet, beaten before the fight begins. I follow him as a sound is followed by an echo. However he moves, I adapt to all his tricks. I'm not conscious of the techniques I use—they just happen by themselves. If a rat is running along a beam or pillar, I can drop it with my stare. However, this monster rat, which came like a ghost and left without a trace, what kind of creature was it?"

The old cat said, "What you have studied depends upon the power of your *ki*, but your approach is flawed because your strength is relative to the situation. You press forward but the enemy presses back: when you press forward and he won't back down, what do you do? You threaten him and he threatens you: when you threaten him and he remains unperturbed, what do you do? Why do you think that you will always be stronger than the enemy?

"Everyone feels their energy is powerful enough to reach the heavens, like the universal energy of Mengzi,* but in reality it's different. His energy derived from the depth of his illumination. This is strength derived from the force of energy. That is why the effect is not the same. His force was like a

---

* Mengzi (Mencius) (372–289 BCE): Confucian philosopher, second only to Confucius in importance.

broad river; yours is like an overnight flood. What do you do when you face someone who won't yield before your *ki*?

"There's a saying: The cornered rat will bite the cat. That is because in his desperate situation, he has nothing to fall back on. He forgets life, forgets desires, forgets winning and losing—he has no thought even of death. His resolve is as strong as steel. How can you hope to defeat someone like this with the strength of your spirit?"

Next, a slightly older grey cat came forward and spoke. "I respect the use of *ki*, but it has physical form, and whatever has form, however subtle, can be seen. For a long time, I have focused on the mind, not using force, not competing, not opposing the enemy's moves. When he is strong, I blend and meet him with harmony. My art is to meet the enemy like a curtain catching a stone. Even a strong rat can find nothing in me to oppose. However, that rat today did not force or yield, it would respond to nothing I did. It came and went like something divine: I have never seen anything like it before."

The old cat said, "What you call harmony is not natural harmony, it comes from your conscious thoughts of harmony. You might avoid the attacking force of your opponent, but if you do so consciously, your opponent can read you. If you try to quiet your mind, your energy is dull, even sluggish. From thinking, then doing, your natural intuitive reactions are impeded, and if that happens, where do you suppose this 'mysterious skill' is going to come from?

"It's simple: think of nothing, do nothing. When I move with intuition I am formless; when I have no form, there is no one in the world who can oppose me.

"However, having said all that, I don't want to imply what each of you has learned is useless. 'The vessels of the Way are all one.' Outer forms contain essential truths. *Ki* is necessary to use the whole body as one. When that energy is uninhibited, you can respond continuously as the situation changes, and when you can blend with the enemy without fighting against his power, even if you are struck with metal or stone, you will escape serious harm.

"But if your thoughts intrude, even a little, you have intention, and your body will not move naturally. Therefore the opponent's mind will not give in to you but continuously oppose you.

"So what is the technique I use? *Mushin*—I naturally respond in a state of 'no-mind.'

"But the way is endless. You shouldn't think that the state I described is the ultimate. Long ago, there was a cat that lived near me. It slept all day and seemed completely listless—it was like a carved wooden statue. No one ever saw it catch anything, yet wherever it was, the area was free of rats. When I visited him to ask the reason, he didn't answer. Four times I asked, and four times there was no answer. It wasn't that he didn't want to answer; he didn't know how to answer. As you know, those who know do not speak; those who speak do not know. This cat had forgotten himself, forgotten the world, and returned to nothingness. He had achieved the state of the divine warrior who does not kill. I have a long way to go to be like him."

Shoken listened to this conversation as if in a dream. Coming forward, he bowed to the old cat and said, "I have been studying the art of swordsmanship for many years but I have yet to attain the true essence. Tonight I listened to everyone's opinions and at last I understood. Please tell me more about its deeper secrets."

The cat replied, "I cannot, for I am just an animal. Rats are my food. What would I know about the affairs of people? However, there are things I have heard in private. Swordsmanship is not something you persevere in just to achieve victory over others. It is also an art through which you can face troubles and clarify issues of life and death. This is an attitude that samurai must always strive to maintain, and so you should master this art. This is why, first, you should concentrate on the principle of life and death, with an unbending will, without doubt or hesitation, using neither cleverness nor calculation; if you can keep your mind calm, dignified and free in its normal state, you can respond without constraint even to constantly changing conditions.

"But when your mind holds some object, however small it may be, it has form—in that moment there is the enemy and there is you, opposed to each other. In this case, you will not be able to adapt to the changing situation spontaneously and skillfully. Your mind will fill with thoughts of death and your self-assurance will be lost: how can you face a decisive contest with confidence? If you win, it will be a blind victory, not one based on the principles of the art.

"To be purposeless is not the same as being aimless. Your mind, originally, has no form, so you should not clutter it with thoughts. When you think about what to do, even a little, your *ki* will move. When your *ki* inclines one way, its flow will not be smooth and unimpeded. It will concentrate in some areas and be lacking elsewhere. You will use too much force where it is concentrated and must be controlled, and not make proper use of the places where it is lacking. Neither will respond as they should.

"What we call 'purposelessness' does not involve 'doing something,' inclining one way or another. No enemy; no self, only following and responding to things as they come, without a trace.

"The I-Ching says, 'No thought, no action; naturally settled, motionless. When it feels, it acts, flowing through the objects and events of the world.' Swordsmen who understand this theory are close to the path."

Shoken then asked, "What is the meaning of 'No enemy, no self'?"

The cat replied, "It is because we are present that there is an opponent. If we are not there, there is no opponent. The term 'enemy' or 'opponent' is one that denotes confrontation. It is the same kind of thing as yin and yang, or fire and water. Whatever has form, has opposition, but if your mind has no form, it can have no opposition. When there is no opposition, there is no opponent. This is called, 'No enemy, no self.' Forgetting both self and object, when you assume a state of poised non-action, you are synchronized—when you break the enemy, you hardly know it. In this state, you are not unaware, but here, where there are no conscious thoughts, you move by intuition.

"When your mind achieves this state of non-action, the world becomes your world. There is no need to cling to strict forms of good and bad. Everyone creates personal distinctions of joy and pain, loss and gain, in their own minds. It is said, 'However wide the world is, there is nothing to seek beyond the confines of your mind.' According to a writer of old, 'When dust gets in your eye, the three worlds seem narrow. When your heart and mind are open, your whole life is enriched.'

"When a tiny grain of sand gets in your eye, you can't open it. It's the same when you get an idea stuck in your mind. Your mind, too, is naturally bright and illuminating, and the same thing will happen when you get something in it.

"It is also said, 'This mind of ours remains ours even if our bodies are torn to pieces in the midst of thousands of enemies. Even the most powerful of enemies cannot take it from us.' Confucius said, 'Even the commonest of men can have an unbreakable will,' and this is exactly why, if we are confused, our mind betrays us.

"I'll stop here. You have to consider things yourselves. This is the way things are passed down from the masters: they can teach theory only. You are the ones who have to get the truth from it. This is called 'self-study,' 'mind-to-mind transmission,' or 'special transmission outside the teachings.' This is not a rejection of teaching: there are just some things a teacher cannot teach. This is not something confined to Zen. In the teachings of holy men or to reach the ultimate in the arts, all of them employ 'mind-to-mind transmission' or 'special transmission outside the teachings.' You must educate yourself. Teaching is just pointing out what you cannot see without help. You are not 'given' anything by the teacher.

It is easy to teach, and easy to hear the words we are taught, but difficult to find it within ourselves and make it our own. This is called 'self-realization.' 'Enlightenment' is waking up to see the dream for what it is. Self-realization is the same. There is no difference."

Sword Theory
(Kensetsu)

Hirayama Shiryu

My swordsmanship is for slaying the enemy brutally. You must use this feeling of ferocity to penetrate directly into the enemy's heart and mind. But what if this killing intent, which should penetrate his core, is missing? I will explain my theory in answer to this.

If you carry a sword or brandish a spear and advance, intent on killing the enemy, the enemy will also pull out his halberd and swing his sword, with the aim of cutting you down. So, you will defend and intercept the enemy's sword and spear, absolutely desperate to preserve your life and keep yourself safe. Make use of this desperation: first, under the enemy's sword you must become a demon; your desire must fan the flames of your vitality and strength of mind and will; at the gates of decision act against your natural inclinations to hesitate, linger, or hang back. There is simply not the leisure to worry that the enemy may harm you. Relax, you can easily prevail over your opponent. How much more so if you have penetrated his mind! If that's so, what's holding you back? It is said, there is no other technique. The warrior's real character is based on his achievements with the blade. It is the path of death, not of life. Even if faced by a mountain of swords or a cave of fire, you should jump for joy and charge in. How much more so when you are cutting with the sword or thrusting with the spear, pure in heart, totally absorbed in certain death, just like a ravenous hawk striking a bird or a starving tiger carrying off its prey. The great lords, too, possess no apprehension or alarm. Penetrate the gate of this unreasoning fear and you will reach a sublime state, independently and freely. In this state the depth to which your urge to kill penetrates far exceeds what you believed possible.

As the Master of Strategy* said, "Those skilled in war control others but are not themselves controlled. He who controls is the host; the one controlled is the guest." It follows that ensuring you are the host, not the guest, is the main principle at the outbreak of war. Regretably, those who lecture on the arts of war in our society sorely need to open their eyes to this. Just receiving and defending, intercepting and obstructing, dodging at the last instant: this is being controlled by others, and it is this that is being a guest. Those who do this well will gain the reputation of having exquisite skills. With these a warrior will never vanquish his opponents. It is thoroughly disgraceful behavior, cowardly and base, to stand a step away from death, and then seek to preserve your life a little longer. And so warriors will soon fall into cowardice: smile if you like, but the schools of swordsmanship all teach this kind of shameless skill. What a sad, sad state of affairs.

If you are only facing an opponent in single combat, a fencer may explain that you can make use of the techniques of blocking, intercepting, and dodging; if two battle formations draw near men stand like a fence or hedge, their spears stick out like a hedgehog's spines and there is nowhere to turn or maneuver. What's more, when frost and snow are the common lot, what good will the blocking, intercepting, and dodging you have learned do you?

---

* Sun Tzu, the legendary strategist of the Warring States period.

Unless you are resolved to put your whole body into your sword and fearlessly thrust it, point and edge, deep into the front ranks of the enemy, how can you reliably lead an assault to crush the enemy's ranks? The enemy will shoot at you with arrows and guns: can those techniques of blocking, intercepting, and dodging help to keep you safe? If they are strong, on the contrary, you will be filled with hesitation and doubt and be unable to meet their attacks. The styles of swordsmen have no theory to cover this situation. Which is to say, they have no answer. Those kinds of schools which deal with single combat fail to address the extent of the warrior's true nature.

According to the theories of the schools of martial arts, if the opponent is strong, you will be beaten; if clumsy, you will win; if your level is the same, you will both die. If this is so, though you spend your life struggling to develop, it is, after all, a useless task. The wise man aims to free himself from the boundaries of skill. If you can bring out your skill, alone and self-reliant, using the body broadly and vibrantly, you will naturally acquire subtlety. Of both Xia Yu* and Meng Ben† who reached this level it is said, "What is there to be afraid of?"

The remark, "engage in ascetic practices with a dauntless spirit," comes from the Buddhist scriptures. It should, in truth, be used to describe the warrior. "Destroy the body and extinguish the soul." This is the design of engaging in ascetic practices with a dauntless spirit. However, attempting to achieve this through sitting in Zen or alternatively through the power of reading (and study), will not give you wisdom; no one can really gain understanding like this. It is useless knowledge. It is clear that practice is what can prevent failure. When I make my students tremble, it is not from this! When we compare it with the sword and spear, which break down both the neglect of and seeking of victory, and deal with the cut and thrust of

---

* Founder of the Xia Dynasty.

† A figure noted for his exemplary courage.

the enemy, as soon as your spirit wavers you assimilate this knowledge into practical understanding. This is called personal experience. If you maintain this attitude, controlling your thoughts over a long period, forging your spirit, avoiding dissipation, hardening your heart against soft sentiments, at last you must come to that stage where your body will not flinch nor your eyes turn away. So, could it not be said you engage in ascetic practices with a dauntless spirit?

When a swordsman chooses the length of his swords, generally it is standard to carry one of two *shaku*, two or three *sun*.* If we stick by this theory, the extra two or three inches allow you to make a follow-up strike. This is not without some truth, but from the start it is misleading. Why indeed, before you have even started it produces an attitude that you may not strike well; if you are only half committed, the opportunity to control the enemy has already been lost. In fact, it just places fetters and chains on the path of the sword. My theory is nothing like this. From the first, it is a given that it contains no contradictions. Therefore there is no discussion of follow-up strikes. By chance, if there is something that is not clear, first stand on bloody ground then do or die. From the start, this is part of it. Ma Kuang† said, "If you don't enter the tiger's lair, you'll never catch the cubs." Sun Tzu said, "If you place your troops on death ground, you will live." The wise man will appreciate this. Therefore for those who are called "strong" on account of their skill, the most important thing is to be deadly serious.

There are some things you can do well if you study and some you can't. The things you can do well without waiting to learn or study are what we might call natural human abilities.

---

* Traditional measures of length. A *shaku* is approximately equal to one foot; 1 shaku equals 10 *sun*.

† Ma Kuang: the older brother of the more well-known Ma Yuan, a Han Dynasty general.

For example, when you stumble, your foot goes out naturally, or when a sharp object comes close to your eyes you blink: you can easily do them without waiting for instruction. This is the wonder of nature. Again, imagine if you push or thrust, your hips don't move and you can't lift your feet. Or when an opponent thrusts or cuts you step in and don't protect your eyes. This would never happen but for your reliance on study and learning. However the schools of martial arts just transmit dodging and intercepting. Why don't they teach how to pierce the enemy with your attacking spirit? Duke Li Wei* said, "Instructing soldiers means teaching them nothing unusual." You will appreciate this.

A Verse of Eight Follies

A secluded life: unaware it does not resemble a jeweled treasure, randomly discussing the mysteries of emperors, kings, and usurpers. This is the first folly.

Soldiers are curbed, war obsolete—to what extent you cannot guess—you have exquisite discourses on the methods of frontal and indirect attacks. This is the second folly.

Three thousand tactics he can call upon in his work; hundreds of weapons to indulge his passion for investigation. This is the third folly.

An old man in his decline calls people together and with the eighteen martial arts he proceeds to boast of his youth. This is the fourth folly.

No one to serve him, cooking and roasting for himself, flesh and clothes both wearing out, murmuring and howling while beating a tub. This is the fifth folly.

---

* Duke Li of Wei (Li Weigong) (571–649): a successful general who served the founder of the Tang dynasty. Also known as Li Jing.

To the northeast, behind my cottage, stands a sheer cliff. Refusing lengthy congratulations and condolences, there I hang from time to time letting loose a yell. That is the sixth folly.

A long sword, six feet in length, concealed in a white rainbow sheath; a huge gun weighing a hundred catties, hidden where the earth was riven by a thunderbolt. This is the seventh folly.

Although my calligraphy falls far short of excellence, desiring an imperial post I forget discussions of peace and war, suffering instead in the halls of power. This is the eighth folly.

The last day of the 9th month, 1821

A Treatise On The Sword
(Kencho)

Hirayama Shiryu

Preface

Hirayama Shiryu said Sima* was an official scholar. He did not have the responsibility of command over even a single soldier. Why was it then, that he carried a sword? A commander shares conditions of hot and cold, hunger and fullness, work and leisure with his officers and men. However, people who discuss the arts only do so in terms of their own style. So in the case of the sword, will you not doubt one person? I myself, as a practitioner, wrote a chapter on sword theory. However, because I included no examples, I feared that people had not been sufficiently able to grasp the truth. Accordingly, I made a careful search through old writings, taking those with suitable examples and wrote a single volume, "A Treatise on the Sword," to show to young people. If a scholar can appreciate the flavor, even in the slightest, and test what is written in them, and can attain the principle of spontaneously entering and exiting, this is how you will know you were not deceived by this old man.

Heigen Hirayama Hisomu Shiryu esq.

---

* Sima Qian (145/135–86 BCE): author of the famous *Shiji* (Records of the Grand Historian), the first Chinese work of biographical history.

Introductory Remarks

The people who discuss the sword in old books don't stop here. But their theories are often highly unusual and of little benefit to students. Therefore I have made this choice. You should be in no doubt of what you see here.

Even though this is not a discussion of original theory of the sword, I found what I hope is a sufficient range of suitable examples and set them out here. In addition, my selection was based on the principle of not expressing morally unsound intentions.

Within the old writings if there were parts expressing the same principles I clarified their ideas before adding them, so the student should use them to direct his thinking.

I have excluded strange tales that have been passed down such as The Maiden of Yue in the *Wu-Yue Spring and Autumn Annals*[*] and the *Sword Tales in Lives of the Immortals*. Readers, please understand.

This is even more true of *Verses of the Secrets of Chousen Swordsmanship*, and the theories of Yu Dayou's *Sword Classic*, recorded in martial compilations, which are all extremely strange and complex. For that reason they were not included. I only included those that require real application.

Set down by Unchu Shinjin

Written by Master Heigen Hirayama
Arranged by Takai Kunimiki, student

---

[*] The official history of the state of Lu from 722–481 BCE. Compiled by Confucius.

Xunzi* in his Discussion of Propriety said, "Those young people who look to life, will most certainly die." This is the same principle as Wuzi's† statement, "Those who seek to hold onto life will lose it." In a contest, those who concentrate on death, who do not seek to preserve their lives, will certainly live.

In Zhuangzi's‡ *Chapter on Ingrained Ideas* it says, "Respond upon feeling, move when you are pressed." "Feeling" means an impression. This relates to the enemy's *sakki* or intention to kill, which penetrates my heart. "Respond" means to synchronize with. It means my mind echoes the enemy's intention to kill. If I synchronize, I can gain the initiative as soon as the enemy's technique begins. "Push" means pressure. "Move" is to act. I take the enemy's sword with my body and from there I strike. Consequently I can take advantage of the tail end of his *ki*. In the *Shuo Yuan's§ Chapter on War* it says, "Duke Shi of Lu responded to the slightest motion of the sword; no sooner had he sensed it than he had already moved. Profound, he adapted endlessly, completely without form." Again, this is the same principle.

In Zhuangzi's *Chapter on Sword Theory* it states, "A good swordsman leaves late, arrives early."

It means, make this five foot shell bait for the enemy, slowly, slowly set your trap: even though he resists, he can't help but strike. Taking advantage of this, as the enemy strikes with his sword, I take the tip of his force, and crush him in an instant—although I begin later, it is as if I was first. It is difficult to express the gist of this either in speech or the written

---

* Xunzi (312–230 BCE): an important early Confucian scholar. Wrote the eponymous work *Xunzi*.

† Wuzi (d.381 BCE): strategist and author of a classic work on strategy.

‡ Zhuangzi (Chuang tzu): important Daoist philosopher; lived around 4th century BCE

§ *Shuo Yuan (Garden of Sayings)*, compiled by Liu Xiang of the Western Han Dynasty.

word. You must acquire this yourself through actual practice. If you misinterpret it you will be trying to move 70 percent or 40 percent through the strike. This is trying to calculate mathematically. When death is but a step away, how can you hope to do this?

In the 9th Verse of the *Songs of Chu** it is written, "Even though you are to lose your head it does not discipline the heart." It is noted that discipline means hurt or pain and is the same as sorrow or regret. However, this is not about just one person. It means, though the head may be separated from the body, the spirit need never fear injury. In a like manner, if the warrior does not prepare his spirit, how can he fulfill his duty on the field of battle?

In Lu Shang's† *Chapter on Troops* it says, "The great decide; they don't waver, and so, act swift as the lightning which gives you no time to cover your eyes, as the thunder which gives no time to cover your ears. Advance like this, take by surprise; act like this, like a madman. Destroy those you strike, all those who approach perish."

If viewed like this, the path of war should have no trace of wavering and hesitation, mistrust and self-doubt, hesitation and indecision. It does not allow for postponing action. In *The Evening Song of the Foxes* it says, "The clever beast turns around to check on its pursuer, and thus it is caught; if the stupid beast turn round to look it trips and the hunter doesn't catch it; the greater your skill, the truer it is." You should grasp the meaning of this verse. If we compare the techniques of the schools of swordsmanship of the long sword, all of them suffer from hesitation and doubt. If you are wise act without constraint.

---

* *Chu Ci*: an anthology of poems compiled during the Warring States period.

† Lu Shang (Jiang Shang): strategist who served the Duke of Zhou, leading to the overthrow of the Shang Dynasty; author of *Six Secret Teachings of Strategy*.

In Wuzi's *Chapter on Motivating Talents* it says, "A single robber with a price on his head, hiding in the open fields, hunted by a thousand men. There is not one who does not look around carefully as if watching for a wolf, each afraid he may be harmed if he rises up in violence. Thus, if one man is willing to lay down his life, one thousand men may be un-nerved." This means if a condemned man is crouched hiding in a wide open field, with a force of one thousand men pursu-ing him, they search as for a ferocious wolf on the prowl: would any man allow himself to be surprised? An outlaw who has decided on certain death would make people afraid he would suddenly burst out and cut them down. This is how one man may terrify a force of a thousand. If you reflect on this, in a single combat situation, if founded on an attitude of certain death, you should crush your opponent, wiping him out like snapping a dry branch. If one man thinks to make a name for himself from his victory, while another, knowing the ground beneath his feet could be his grave, advances step by step, the difference between them is immense.

In Wei Liaozi's* *Chapter on Discussion of Organization* it says, "One warrior lays about him with his sword: in the mid-dle of a city of ten thousand people there is not one who will not seek safety. The reason is not that one man has courage and all the rest are unworthy. Rather it depends on whether they aim to live or die." In the *Han Fei Zi*† it says, "If there is one man with the courage to die, he can face ten men, ten can face one hundred; one hundred can face one thousand; one thousand can face ten thousand and with ten thousand

---

* Wei Liaozi: author of the work of the same name; one of the 7 Military Clas-sics of ancient China. Written during the period of the Warring States (403–221 BCE).

† The teachings of Han Fei Zi (ca280–233 BCE), an important philosopher of the Legalist school.

you can conquer the world!" In Master Lu's* *Chapter on Intimidation* it says, "Zhan Shu vowed to die for Lord Tian, thus the whole kingdom of Qi was afraid. Yu Rang's promise to die for Xiang Zi awed the whole Zhao clan. The death of Cheng Xing affected the King of Han. All the people of Zhou trembled." They all illustrate this principle. In the *Biography of Kuai Dong*† it says, "The hesitation of a fierce tiger is no match for a hornet's sting. If Mou Han suffered from doubt, he would be no match for a desperate child." It's not that tigers and wolves are not fierce or that Mou Han was not brave. However if they hold back or hesitate, exhibit fear and misgivings and cannot wholeheartedly embark on an enterprise unnerved, it will not be enough. On the contrary, what is fearsome about a wasp's sting, or the thrust of a short sword from a child, is whether they advance or not. A warrior should be aware of this. Now that the time has come to match spears and the thrust of swords as a matter of a life or death, you delay and retreat, or turn and look back, to-ing and fro-ing, everyone lingers here. That's why my blaze of murderous spirit and energy is never put forth; that brilliance of divine origin doesn't pierce the enemy's mind. Already in the demon world and more, to keep the happiness of your short life, shrinking in the shadow of your short sword, hoping to hide behind the shaft of your spear. This base cowardliness of spirit is not worth spitting on. By these means you will reap defeat, leaving shame on your corpse. My comrades in arms, I pray you escape this demon world and enter the transcendent state of spiritual martial power.

---

* Lu Buwei (d.235 BCE), was regent and Chancellor during the minority of Qin Shi Huangdi, the first Qin emperor. Sponsored the compilation of the *Lushi chunqiu* (*Master Lu's Spring and Autumn Annals*).

† Kuai Dong was advisor to Han Xin, general of Liu Bang, the founding emperor of the Han Dynasty.

The *Sima Fa** says, "To wield the blade you must be fast."

Mao Yuanyi[†] said, "To win when you cross blades, the soldier must be resolute and quick."

Long ago, when the soldier was already associated with the sword, slowness and hesitation were seen as cowardly, retreat as self-interest. When broken of this selfishness, decision, speed, and resolution will stand out. It is as if a hungry hawk snatches a bird; like a ravenous tiger seizing its prey. When you have achieved this you will have to carefully keep this in check yourself. It is much the same as rolling a round boulder down a steep slope. Sun Tzu, the Sage of Strategy, passed down the following, "I have heard of strategy that is quick but clumsy, but I have never seen good strategy that was long and drawn out." This is for the same reason. It is also said, "Once considered and decided, the mind is strong, movement free of doubt."

Once you have firmly decided that you face certain death, overwhelming thoughts of fear will be exhausted in your mind and you will yourself create a spirit of valor and firmness. So you will advance and withdraw in time with the opportunity, you can achieve by yourself the marvelous state of your own (perfect) judgment. Why be troubled by doubts? For "advance" we can say to face the enemy and press forward. For "withdraw," kill the enemy and return. Advance, cut down the opponent, afterward pull back—there is nothing more than this. This is the principal of advance and withdrawal. If it should so happen that the enemy is strong, so it might be said we were allowed to advance and forced to retreat, this is not advancing and withdrawing yourself. This is a very great error in principle.

---

* *Sima Fa* (*Methods of The Minister of War*): a military work attributed to Tian Rangju, Minister of the State of Qi during the Spring & Autumn Period.

† Mao Yuanyi (1594–1640): compiler of the *Wubei Zhi*, a Ming Dynasty military encyclopaedia.

In Master Lu's *Chapter on Loyalty and Honesty*, Yao Li[*] says, "A knight only suffers when lacking bravery. Why not when lacking skill?"

What this means is that a knight who suffers lack of courage should consider it an illness. If he has no desire for distinction he would not worry. When battle comes, could he go forward to be the first to match spears, the first to scale the walls: facing the massed spearheads of the enemy forces arrayed like reeds, to be thrust at and stabbed for the sake of a reward?—would a desire to receive commendation as the "foremost spear" be a sufficient inducement? Likewise the title of "first to scale the walls," is not reason enough to climb in the face of the enemy obstructions, to brave concealed arrows, spears coming from loopholes, being shot at by guns. For anyone who plans to scale the castle gate, there are all kinds of dangers: you are struck at and cut, spears and naginata are thrust out from behind sandbags. Would anyone enter such chaos to storm the walls if they had the idea of returning successfully? In both these cases, in our desperate situation, knowing that this is the time to repay the debt to your state, if you don't step in you will never stand out. With such resolution, though surrounded by ten thousand dead, you can be the one who lives; you can gain success and distinction too, but as I said previously, do not depend on it. However, today, though you may be thin as a pair of fire tongs, without the strength to lift a bale of rice, do your utmost as a samurai, and if your courage is firm you can ride out against a thousand men. But if your courage is not firm, though you may have great strength and skill, a warrior of unmatched stature even, you will not be fearsome at all. People will think nothing of you. Incidentally, Yao Li appeared in *Wu-Yue Spring and Autumn Annals*. He was a small war-

---

* Yao Li: an assassin in the Spring and Autumn period who went to great lengths to prove his trustworthiness to his intended target, committing suicide after his mission was successful.

rior and not strong, so weak he could be blown over by a stiff wind, yet he stabbed to death the brave but oppressive Prince Qingi. Truly this should be the whetstone which polishes the warrior's heart.

In the *Huainanzi*,* in *The Art of the Leader* it states, "For the warrior there is nothing sharper than the mind. Even Mo Ye† is inferior." In the original notes, "sharp" means effective. To strike with total concentration is most effective. That means there is nothing that can crush the enemy's heart and soul as effectively as your spirit. Mo Ye's famous sword is no match.

This is the theory of mental attack, mental battle of Ma Su‡ of Szechwan. If you can see the opponent's root is crushed you can ignore the leaves and branches as being defeated. Techniques of the hands are leaves and branches. The spirit is the root. If the enemy's spirit is broken, techniques which he performs with his hands alone will not help. Standing in the pure uncluttered state of certain death (the realm of samadhi), with no care for your body, the hope, the desire to kill the opponent, the mindset and vigor to face anything, to go straight ahead, directly penetrating and piercing the enemy's mind, making him tremble and quake, your highly perfected techniques will be of no use. When you have achieved this, one thousand swords as sharp as Gan Jiang and Mo Ye will not be your equal. I am not the only one to know this. There are undoubtedly those who have already glimpsed this truth. Therefore I added this appendix to complement the ideas in my original work, and have them published together like this.

---

* *Masters of Huainan*: compiled under the direction of the King of Huainan in the 2nd century BCE, a Taoist influenced compendium of philosophy and lore.

† Mo Ye (usually mentioned together with her husband, Gan Jiang): famous swordsmiths during the Spring & Autumn Period. The names were also given to a pair of famous swords they made: Mo Ye was the female or yin sword, and Gan Jiang the yang sword.

‡ Ma Su (190–228): military strategist for the Kingdom of Shu during the Three Kingdoms period.

Certainly it is not to boast of my esteem. It is just for students to consider and refer to.

The *Sou Shen Ji*[*] tells of how Xiang Quzi[†] of Chu, journeying at night, saw a boulder lying on the ground. Mistaking it for a crouching tiger, he fitted an arrow to his bow and shot at it, burying the forged metal head and the whole arrow up to its flights. Upon inspection he realized that it was a rock. When he shot at it later, his arrowheads failed to make an impression. Also in China there was Li Guang,[‡] the governor of You Bei Ping. Similarly, the tiger he shot turned out to be a stone. Liu Xiang[§] said, "If you are wholehearted, even metal and rock will part. This depends on the situation and the person. You cannot chant in harmony or follow the movements if you are not completely unified, inside and out." (From the *Bo Wuzhi*[¶]– *Supplementary Chapter on History*).

In a similar vein to the above, the King of Chu was in his garden where there was a white monkey. Being a talented archer, he shot at the monkey, but though he shot many arrows the monkey laughed and swatted them aside. So the King sent for Youji.[**] Youji had no sooner touched his bow than the monkey clung to the tree, whimpering in fear.

In the period of the Six Kingdoms, Geng Lei[††] is held to have said to the king of Wei, "Your humble retainer can bring down a bird even though he shoots without an arrow." The

---

[*] *Records of Spirits* by Gan Bao (d.336): a collection of stories of the supernatural.

[†] Famous as an archer in the Zhou Dynasty.

[‡] Li Guang (d.119 BCE): famous general of the Han Dynasty; also noted for his skills in archery.

[§] Liu Xiang (79-08 BCE): Confucian scholar; editor of, among other things, the *Shuo Yuan*, mentioned above.

[¶] *Record of the Investigation of Things*: compiled by Zhang Hua (265-316).

[**] Yang Youji was a famous archer of the state of Chu who lived during the Spring Autumn period.

[††] Geng Lei: a famous archer from the State of Wei, who lived during the Warring States Period.

King replied, "If that's so you should be able to show me here and now." "That should be possible," Geng Lei replied. In a little while they heard the cries of geese flying from the east. Geng Lei shot and the bird was brought down. (This appears in the *Huainanzi* in the *Chapter on Wide Learning*). These are all examples of the ability to penetrate with the strength of the spirit. I hope students appreciate them.

In the 12th chapter of the *Wei Laozi*, *The Mausoleum*, it states that "The victorious army is like water. Though water is soft and weak, its touch can cause cliffs to crumble—there is nothing strange about this. Acting only according to its nature, it does indeed need only to touch." What this means is that the victorious army is like water. What it touches is broken and defeated. That something soft and weak like water with its touch will cause a dry cliff to crumble is because the nature of water is to follow one path and thus its touch is pure. A warrior should sense this intuitively. Those who learn the arts and crafts of the warrior nowadays, no sooner face their opponent than they feint to the right and strike to the left, feint low and strike high. Without exception they lure and deceive so the killing energy never strikes into the enemy's guts, transfixing him, thus leaving him unaffected and, furthermore, free to move around as he likes. How sad, how very sad. And so, though you spend a lifetime of bitter hardship, in the end you will die still dreaming of that pleasant life, unable to get on in the world. It is my hope that, by taking the principle of water which, in being true to its own nature, can cause cliffs to crumble at its touch, you will wake up to reality. If you use your true spirit to act authentically, independently and self-reliantly entering that mysterious state, the enemy cannot meet your steely glare, the light of which is blinding as the morning sun.

In the *Huainanzi's Explanation of Strategy* it says, "You may shut out the wind and rain, but heat and cold cannot be let in or kept out, for they are formless." Wind and rain have form: you may shutter them out. But for formless heat and cold, though you shut them out they cannot be prevented from entering, nor can you open the shutters and let them out. Similarly, swords are like human wind and rain which the opponent may intercept and obstruct, receiving each attack so his body is untouched. The power of the spirit which is, in human terms heat and cold, can easily penetrate the enemy's heart; if you crush his spirit, how can he put up a defense? Furthermore, in the *Lu Shang* it says, "The void can penetrate where there is no opening." This is the same principal.

In the same work, does it not say, "When you cross blades with an opponent, though no different in skill, the braver is sure to win, because he acts with greater integrity"? Victory or defeat is not a matter of skill, but of bravery and cowardice. Thus a brave man will not be distracted by fear and so is single-minded. It is through this that he can secure victory. Those who discourse on martial arts these days are not like this. For them victory and defeat are a matter of skill. Thus it is a foregone conclusion that you will beat someone who is inferior to you, lose to someone who is superior, and if you are both equal, you will both die. In this way, you can labor for years, for a whole lifetime, to no effect. This is only the narrow view exhibited by most styles.

In *Essays of the Late Ming* it talks of the Incident of 1449[*] (The time of the Northern Raid of the Ming Emperor Yingzong), when an invitation went out to all the brave men of the empire. Answering this, one Li Tong of Shanxi came to the capital where he was made a chief instructor. He was tested in all 18 weapons and named best of all, but when rewards were

---

[*] Incident of 1449: The invasion by Oirat Mongols, which provoked a spectacularly incompetent defense by the Ming Chinese under the leadership of the eunuch Wang Zhen, involving heavy losses and the capture of the Emperor. The Oirats were unable to capitalize on their success.

to be given for their deeds against the enemy, he was not among those chosen. Though lower ranked soldiers were recognized for their deeds, why did Tong's name not appear? Looking at this we cannot argue that winning and losing is a matter of skill. That's why since long ago, we never hear of the deeds in battle of men praised for their skill with the sword and spear. Inadome Ichimu* was an expert with the musket; he could hit a willow leaf at a hundred paces, and standing in a thatched cottage, could, without fail, shoot birds perched on the rooftop by the sound of their voices alone. Despite his great skill, when facing the enemy in the Korean War,† he did not hit with a single shot. (This can be found in the *War Chronicles of the Keicho Era*, written by Gyokuteki Inken). Thus victory and defeat is never decided by skill in technique. Yet there is no way, save by beginning the study of the martial arts by which to develop this controlled anger and killing spirit. It is solidified by the study of the art and techniques. But if it is left at the level of wisdom learned from books, you will never avoid defeat in real situations. This book learned art is called lip-service strategy. I'm not saying people should not study these arts. I just regret that the way cannot be grasped through these discourses. How sad, how very sad. In this whole country there is not one great man to step forward and put an end to these corrupt habits and wake us from these deluded practices.

In *Liezi's*‡ *Chapter on Huangdi*§ it says, "If a drunk falls from a carriage even though he may be hurt, he will not be killed. Although people's bones and joints are the same, the

---

* Inadome Ichimu (Sukenao) (1552–1611): founder of the Inadome-ryu of firearms. Served the Hosokawa family before transferring his loyalties to the Tokugawas. Later appointed artillery master of the Edo bakufu.

† Japan's ill-advised invasion of Korea (1592).

‡ *Liezi*: a Taoist text attributed to Lie Yukou (5th century BCE) but more likely to have been compiled during the 4th century CE.

§ The legendary Yellow Emperor, founder of China.

one who suffers the injury is different. In this case the spirit is whole." Though a drunk who falls from a carriage may suffer minor injuries, he does not die, helped by his obliviousness to danger; his mind is unafraid for it is full. For a warrior engaged in combat, so completely full of spirit that fears are driven out of his head, arrows and musket balls should not hit him. In the strategic writings of the Kenshin-ryu* it says, "Truly aimed arrowheads will not stick in, the shield at my side will be pierced through the center." This is also the same. In Laozi's work it says, "Those skilled in cultivating life will not encounter the *zhi*† (unicorn) or the tiger; though he enter a body of troops, he will not be struck. There is no place for the zhi to thrust its horn, or the tiger to lodge its claws, or for the soldier to insert his blade." Why is this so? It is because he has no place of vulnerability. Similarly in the *Bo Wuzhi* it says, "The crane achieves its longevity because it has no stagnant energy within." All have the same idea. It is based on enlightened calm and spirited movement. Students, here is the way to enlightenment, use it to grasp and manipulate the opportunities of life.

Takai Yoshitarou
Kojima Kenjirou
Katayama Shinzaburou
Kamei Kinshirou
The whole school

---

* Kenshin-ryu: the school of strategy associated with Uesugi Kenshin, the famous Sengoku Period warlord of Echigo.

† *Zhi* is often translated as rhinoceros, but the animal in question is more correctly a legendary one-horned "goat-antelope," possibly derived from the Vietnamese *saola*.

Afterword

When I was a boy I studied martial arts with my teacher for a number of years but owing to my stupid nature, I did not get the hang of even one of what are known as the eighteen weapons. Of special note was this book I received. I read deeply and pondered its meaning from morning till night, not relaxing in my studies. Later, I was engaged in official duties for some thirty years, but ever careful not to be lost in solitary doubt, I still didn't give up reading and so benefitted greatly. So why is it only swordsmen and warriors who have the advantage of this book? Now for my son and friends, it is my intention to find a proofreader, publish, and share this book. Which is, in short, the reason why I'm writing this.

The 3rd year of Meiji (1870) winter, the 10th Month
Respectfully written by Takai Kunimiki, student

Joseishi's Discussions
On The Sword
(Joseishi Kendan)

Matsuura Seizan

There is a right way and a wrong way to wield the sword. If you wield it wrongly you will not achieve victory, because this way is false.

I tell those who are having difficulty with the speed of techniques to counter slowly. If they stick to this approach, even though the technique is not fast to begin with, it will eventually speed up. Mengzi said, "When Yi* taught people to shoot, he would always draw the bow fully. His students also strove to draw the bow to its full extent. A master craftsman always uses a compass and square when teaching. His students also use a compass and square." This example does not depart from the principle in the slightest.

When you are being taught what is good and bad in swordsmanship you should realize these words may spell the difference between victory and defeat. But what you cannot know is your master's personal style and understanding.

In striking from the upper guard have the feeling that the point of your sword will cut right down to the crotch.

---

* A legendary archer of incomparable skill.

Thrust at a fly you have tethered by a fine hemp thread. This is also the spirit of swordsmanship.

If you are interested in the inner depths of swordsmanship consider this: first you unsheath the sword you normally wear at your waist and stand facing the enemy, who will do likewise. Now you must think like a reckless man. If you can capture this feeling, do not deviate from it in the slightest. This is how you can penetrate the depths of this art.

Anyone who doubts the words of their teacher, however slightly, will surely fail to master the inner secrets of their art. However, my master said someone who believes in sword techniques that can overcome canons will never master those secrets either.

You may expend much time in an effort to attain skill with the sword, but if you do not look at your life as a whole, you will soon reach old age and despite all, find yourself old and unskilled. You may chant the Nembutsu with no knowledge of the Pure Land, but how much steeper the path to Buddha must be. These are the rewards for mistaking the path.

When you take up a wooden sword to strike with the *set-suka-to* (armor splitting technique) and raise it in the upper position, don't watch the opponent's sword, enter the state of *mushin* (no-mind). When you strike the opponent's sword, it is like the instant a spark triggers a musket: abandon your judgment and strike down as if wielding the divine power of Marishiten or one of the gods. If you feel as if you are using your own power, it will not be enough. You should reflect on this attitude.

Generally, with regard to the grip of the striking hand, you should shout as you strike: *uchi-oshi* when you're advancing and *uchi-hiku** when you pull back. If you do this, you will naturally remember the grip. Using a cleaver the same way as you use a fish knife is a mark of inexperience. Again, when

---

* *Uchi* means strike. *Oshi, hiku*: push and pull, respectively.

you strike with sword technique called *ya-uchi-ken*, when you cut you should have the feel of the dragonfly's tail as it skims across the water.

In swordsmanship, someone who uses an unusual technique will steal a victory over someone who was not expecting it. This is because the practitioner's understanding is poor. The reason I say this is that the movements of a person's arms and legs are always limited, and there is no one who is an exception. If you add to this the two swords, there should be no mystery about this or that technique. If you understand that everybody's arms and legs conform to these limitations, and are aware of the full extent of their movement, you will see that, of course, they follow the same rule, and the secret transmissions are also things that you can generally understand by yourself.

You should not judge what you have heard just now. Think on it deeply, and when you have come to a level of understanding, you will undoubtedly come to believe these words. As you have single-mindedly applied yourself since you began your studies, you must have researched as thoroughly as you could. Thorough research means testing yourself in matches whenever you have the chance.

If we speak of the grip for cutting, with the face of the hilt leading, at the moment of contact you should have the feeling of using your grip to stop.

The long sword can be used in one hand. The grip for this requires you to exert the strength of the wrists and the bottom of the feet together forcefully at the instant you strike. This includes the long sword technique *ransha* among others.

If you take the length of a sword, with a blade of two shaku two sun, and divide it into ten, one of these divisions would be two sun, two *ho*.* Of this, a single inch of blade decides victory or defeat. Furthermore, you can win using only a

---

* One tenth of a *sun*: approx. 0.3 cm or 0.1 in.

fourth or fifth of that. If you ponder on the spirit of sword techniques, you will be able to understand this. What's more, when cutting with the area near the tip, the cutting edge in a long sword is between four or five sun and seven or eight sun. This is for when the enemy attacks by surprise—you can cut with this part even though your hands are pressed in. Cut with a pulling cut as you crouch.

The technique known as *seigan* is *yang*; *marubashi* is *yin*. For *seigan* you should probably use the point. The blade may be insufficient. For *marubashi* you should probably use the blade: the point may not be enough.

The arts of drawing the sword, swordsmanship, *yawara**— all of them have established their own lineages and become separate arts. Though that is so, of course drawing the sword blends into swordsmanship. *Yawara* is also one corner of swordsmanship. Those who study swordsmanship in depth will, of course, be beaten by the enemy if they don't realize this. You should think hard about this.

Confucius once said, "Aspire to the way, build on virtue, practice benevolence, find your recreation in the arts." If you aspire to swordsmanship, build on form, practice the mind, find your recreation in the sword.

The kodachi is a short sword and has, from the start, been one path of swordsmanship. The staff, cane, iron fan, though none of them have blades, if you attain proficiency in their use they all share the same principle as the sword, like water from the same source.

There are three paths by which you may reach the inner teachings. They are:

mind, form, sword;
form, sword, mind;
sword, form, mind.

---

* *Yawara* is an old term for what is more commonly known as *jujutsu*.

When you are to fight in a contest, it is not good to be proud. Nor is it good to be humble. Maintaining a steady mind, you should simply hold the thought that this is a win or lose situation.

When you use a particular technique, there are sometimes instances when you do it again to get it right. If this is to ensure the form is technically perfect, then this is not, in fact, in the true spirit of swordsmanship. Your aim should be to respond freely to changes in the situation, and so each technique must have variations. If you don't understand this, you are not learning the art of the sword. There are people whose bodies move in unexpected ways, so there are many occasions when it is impossible to plan your responses in advance. At such times you should move as your spirit dictates. If you feel ashamed that this improvised technique is not true to the rules of the style, your attitude is, in fact, like someone that doesn't know the spirit of the style. In order to adapt to the demands of real situations, to respond to the unexpected, there are many occasions when you win using an improvised technique. However, if you feel shame when you use a technique like that and feel it requires correction, if you immediately re-established your distance of engagement, there is no shame in it, no matter how unorthodox it is. You should have the attitude that all your skills are for use in combat.

This is the flavor of attack: as soon as his fuse touches your priming pan, you should already think of it as the roar from the muzzle. "He" is the enemy. The "fuse" is compared to movement. The "priming pan" refers to your mind. The "roar" is the attack that is launched and reaches him.

This is the flavor of winning with the technique *seigan no tachi*: extend the *ki* from the base of the sword (*tsuba moto*) through the blade to the tip. You should project this *ki* from the tip to strike the enemy. The technique is the sword; if you think victory lies outside the sword, you have little skill.

Asked about the soul of Japan,
The scent of wild cherry blossoms
In the morning sun.

I heard that when Motoori Norinaga* wrote these lines above a painting someone who read it praised it as a masterpiece, saying, "It is not that I can't understand the ideas it contains, but I cannot fathom the way you have compressed them into a single verse." Therefore, applying the above to swordsmanship, boasting my style differs from other styles, my style is better than other styles is, after all, a mark of inferior swordsmanship. In the preface to the *mokuroku*† it says, "It is as if there is, at the core, no conflict." This is the real spirit of what Norinaga expresses in his verse. If you can understand this saying and the idea, you should be able to appreciate the essential nature of victory and defeat.

In the *Mei Chu*,‡ there is an extract from *The Discourses of Chu*, taken from the *Guoyu*§ which says, "The ruler (Heaven) is concerned with war, the government (earth) with civil affairs, the nation with loyalty." This is the top level of human affairs, but it corresponds to the upper levels of swordsmanship. This is because we can relate the upper guard (*jodan*) to heaven, the lower guard (*gedan*) to earth, while the nation is the "middle path." When the sword is in *jodan*, it strikes down with no delay—a finishing blow. In *gedan* too, of course, the sword is fast, and you can use it to stop him by adapting to his changes. With the sword in the middle path, if you are not

---

* Motoori Norinaga (1730–1801): Japanese *kokugaku* scholar—this school of thought reoriented study towards Japanese rather than Chinese classics.

† A catalogue of techniques, usually presented as a certificate of achievement by the head of a school of martial arts. In this case it is referring to Joseishi's *mokuroku* that he received from his teacher.

‡ A collection of Chinese works with commentaries by Minagawa Kien.

§ *Guoyu*: a compendium of the histories of various states from the Western Zhou to the Wu, including the *Discourses of Chu*.

loyal, if you harbor the slightest doubt as to the sword technique, you will not win. This is the principle of nature.

Among the secrets of victory and defeat there is the *yariai-tachi* (spear matching sword). You can use it wielding a long sword. Of course, you can use it wielding a short sword. You can apply it with two swords. The two sword techniques were devised by the founder, Josuiken. Anyway, you should be aware of the immense advantage it gives. It should be a winning technique. However everyone does this kind of technique on the surface, so it will not truly decide victory or defeat. Take a spear and test for yourself what makes the difference between winning and losing. Students tend to simply keep secrets as they are, admiring the beauty of the technique. If you don't test whether or not you have real ability with a technique, even though you saw how your teacher invariably used it with success, it is not yours. In the end it is something you must chase, bring down, and capture. You must think on this deeply.

The advanced sayings of swordsmanship speak of *aiki*—a harmonious contest. What exactly is it? Is it any different from the *aiki* of harmonious mind? If it is not, the harmonious mind may be something you have already heard of as a part of the normal spirit of the sword. I cannot answer. Without speaking for other schools, in our school, rather than first using the wooden sword, we use a *shinai* for practicing basic techniques. Until reaching the advanced levels of techniques that we teach, all the techniques have the same spirit. The spirit of the *uchidachi* (attacker) is that you will be hit, even by beginners. This gradually changes when people have developed some degree of skill and embark on hard training. However, as you use the advanced skills that have been handed down, for the *uchidachi*, this is sufficient as an assessment of skill. This is *aiki*. When accomplished people speak of *aiki* it is difficult to grasp their meaning.

Even though swordsmanship is composed of techniques

with the sword, if you are unarmed, you will be far more effective than those who are armed with a sword but greatly neglect its use. If you can grasp this attitude and foster it in daily life without deviating from your goal, you should really reach the deeper levels.

Those who use swordsmanship learn how to wield the sword to achieve victory. From this it is necessary to learn the principle of assessing the body. For this reason, in our Shingyoto-ryu, in the end the sword becomes part of the body.

While swordsmanship is, of course, composed of hand techniques, to use them the legs are required. You should be aware that this is what you should concentrate on to develop your technique. For this reason if we want to know if they are skilled or not we should pay more attention to a person's feet than their hands. Someone who uses their legs in concert with their body will certainly win. In our school's transmission on victory and defeat, it also says three parts of training should deal with the lower body.

Previously I mentioned what is called unarmored swordsmanship. What exactly is it? This term refers to someone who is empty handed. It can also refer to not wearing armor. For example, even though you are unarmored, if you are armed, you should be able to win. If you were wearing steel, empty hands would be useless against you. If so it would not be called naked swordsmanship. In the place of the empty hand there is swordsmanship. Someone who has completely thought this out is someone who is really accomplished in this art.

Someone who is learning the sword should watch people who have developed their mind and for this reason you should watch as much as you can at the training hall. Indeed, what is called swordsmanship, may be taken as a cultural way, because without the sword it is completely mental, and so it is always important to store up knowledge on the sword and short sword. In another case, for those who are recommended to accompany their father, older brother, or master, it is necessary to be familiar with etiquette. Because this etiquette stems from the spirit of vigilance, if you perform this duty well, it will also carry over to the heart of swordsmanship. Those who feel they can't understand this roundabout explanation do not have the real spirit of swordsmanship. But when it is time to impart the *himitsu ken* teachings from the inner teachings of our school, those who have resolved to maintain this excellent spirit of caution in daily life will already have the necessary attitude and approach. Those who are seen to display hesitation will not be inducted into the teachings of *himitsu ken*.

Do not think that winning is simply a matter of cutting the enemy. You should think that victory is not allowing the enemy to cut you. If you fail to think like this, you will not be able to attain victory.

If asked what the rationale is for a giving a certificate (*inka*) based on testing, by way of illustration I would say you should look as far as you can see. If you were woken from the depths of a drunken sleep, you would not have the alertness to adapt to an unexpected situation. You should think about this. You should know that those who always do well are people who have attained the ability to adapt. There is no other occasion for awarding certification.

This is the spirit of the swordsman: whenever you are doing something like drinking, entertaining women, or just listening to the koto, if somebody attacks you from behind, you must be ready to cut them down immediately. You should always strive to maintain this spirit in everyday life.

In swordsmanship, when you see a person move, you should be able to guage the level they have attained. This is because anyone who is always bumping their heads on things, sticking their behinds into things behind them as they turn round, grabbing onto sliding doors to help them stand, stumbling over stationary objects, or slipping over in muddy streets is someone without a trained spirit. Therefore, in swordsmanship, whenever you see how a person moves you will know their level.

The long sword technique called *fuushin-tou* is extremely closely guarded and imparted when the student is ready to be granted a license (*menkyo*). The character for "wind" is used for *fuu*. Coming from an older sword technique which had no fixed shape (*mukei*), it is formless. Although our school has a liking for such things, all the major sword techniques have form. Like all the rest, this technique also has its own unique form. Be that as it may, though you have reached the level to be taught this technique, if your determination to progress is not strong enough, it is difficult to understand. A short while ago, I was looking through the *Kokin Waka Shu*,* and saw a verse that went:

I can see a thousand colors
Blowing in the wind.
Did the leaves of Autumn trees
Know they would fall?

You should understand what this verse means. Winning by *fuushin* is something that cannot be forseen by the opponent. They will only realize they have lost after you have won. As with the technique itself, I cannot say if you are ready to learn. When you reach the level of *fuushin no jutsu*, you should use the meaning of this verse to see. I wrote this for people at the limits of their learning, and for those who aspire to this way.

Nowadays, when I see the way people handle their sword in daily life, from watching how they deal with it generally, whether they place it down heavily or not, how they take it

---

* An early Heian period collection of poems, sponsored by the Emperor Daigo.

out of their sash, it is easy to see the results of not being alert. Common people may exhibit awareness of this kind of thing but those learning swordsmanship must take special care to do so. After all, though you carry two swords, this was originally a matter of caution. It was not for the sake of etiquette. Lack of awareness is visible. Has everyone's spirit declined so much?

When you are learning swordsmanship, among the various types of voices you use there is the empty (kyo) cry and the full (jitsu*) cry. Of course the empty cry is bad and the full cry good. However much you practice this cry you will not be able to gain adequate skill. Therefore you should work at keeping the full cry in your breast and not letting out the empty cry. You should realize that someone who can neither distinguish these empty and full cries by ear nor understand the difference, is someone who doesn't yet understand the intent of swordsmanship.

In the sayings of Confucius it states, "A superior man does not hold a man in higher estimation because of his words, nor does he hold his words to be of lesser value because of who he is." This can be applied to swordsmanship. In Master Jochishi's† sayings it is written "In terms of techniques, the theory of complete impartiality applies to the movement of the arms, legs, mind, and body. To apply this theory to the trajectory of the sword, it is necessary to have developed the sinews to move correctly. If you have not practiced, you will not have the sinews to enable you to move correctly." This is surely true. Therefore it is true of a swordsman that if he cannot do with his hands what he says, or what he does is not what he says he can do, he has not reached the highest levels.

---

* *Kyo-jitsu*: literally meaning empty and full, this concept is an important one in traditional martial arts. *Jitsu* often refers to the presence of energy or intention in a part of a body or a movement, and *kyo* the lack thereof. These qualities can change very quickly and one is not necessarily more desirable than the other.

† Jochishi: Shingyoto-ryu master and teacher of Jokeishi.

The deeper teachings of the sword are nothing. If you believe that someone who has achieved a degree of mastery would remain undefeated even if drunk, as they would be if drinking sweet sake, this is something I had better address. In case it is said I am unskilled in this art on account of my shallow learning, I received the seal of my teacher Jokeishi.* Thus, I can say flatly you shouldn't mix with commonplace students. Though I do not know the person, I should be able to read their intentions. If you are attacked while under the influence of drink and somehow find yourself in this dire situation, your mind abandoned to pleasure, the speed of your hands and feet will lessen, and you will be largely unable to read your opponent, and then, well! what techniques do you have that will secure you victory? From the first, said Master Zesuiken,† even if these are your boon companions you should avoid this kind of situation. Therefore in the assorted documents of transmission in the Shingyoto-ryu passed down to me by Jokeishi, it states: "If someone has studied hard under you for a number of years and through exhaustive studies has advanced beyond technique and theory, to say nothing of their devoted behavior, they are ready for certification. To receive a license, a certificate, or to be granted knowledge of XX (the name of a sword technique—as it is a restricted technique it is not recorded here), and from there go on to further transmissions, as well as showing devotion to practice, which is taken for granted, this person should be gentle and sincere. Even if they are superior in ability they must not be approved if their behavior is not correct, if they are not both determined and truly sincere."

The teacher should enforce this rule strictly. You should therefore look at this carefully. Whoever you transmit the

---

* Jokeishi: Joseishi's teacher in the Shingyoto-ryu.
† Zesuiken: Iba Zesuiken Hideaki (1648–1717), founder of the Shingyoto-ryu.

deeper aspects of the art to, you must make sure their character and behavior is unimpeachable. If they are prone to occasional bouts of drinking, they must keep this within limits. Anyway, you should get a good sense of this. Here is another story. There was formerly a warrior of the Lord of Ushu Shounai named Ishikawa Idayuu* who was the official teacher of swordsmanship. On one occasion while he was out he got extremely drunk. On the return route, he walked back unsteadily, quite unlike his normal self, unable to keep to the middle of the street. As I followed along I thought about how he always spoke of swordsmanship. Now, if someone were to attack there's no doubt it would be difficult for him to react. If that's so, it makes it difficult to fathom the depths of this technique. I couldn't come to any clear conclusion about it, and we returned to the master's house. Referring back to it, the master said to me, "On today's outing you must have really been watching closely as you followed me. I guess at times you thought, 'Ah! I have a chance to beat him.' But you shouldn't be content until you know what people are hiding. If you think about this, you should understand. Those skilled in other schools share the same opinion."

For swordsmanship you should indeed think that crossing swords is extremely important, but this is something you come to later. For now you should pass it over, and not get involved in anything—you have to realize that there is something that comes first. You should make sure you understand what this means. For example, a gun is something that can even smash through strong armor, so it is natural to approach it with some trepidation. But piercing the target is only the final stage. To get there, to smash through something, first you have to hit it: everybody wants to try again if they miss. So, for the very reason that it is so nerve-wracking, you need to have this

---

* Ishikawa Idayuu: swordmaster of the Shinkyu-ryu.

kind of determination before you even fire it. I hope you can follow my reasoning.

Don't speak of swordsmanship in terms of a technique for a single person. In addition there is swordsmanship for two people, three people, four, five, or ten people. Beyond this, you can extrapolate to numbers even as great as one hundred. If you ask how you can do this, the answer is from the stories other people tell. Someone who does not pay attention to the experience of other people and aspires only to perfect their own movement will not get far in swordsmanship. In a situation where you are accompanying your lord, or your father, or older brother, you should focus on them exclusively.

Now there are many schools of swordsmanship. These stem from each respective founder's specialties from among the techniques he had mastered. Therefore if you manage to perfect the principles of the sword the schools become one. You will understand this as you amass training. So now, though some students may say that within the many schools, there are those which are better or worse, this shows they don't understand the reality of the situation. When they come to blows, whatever the school, the better man will win. In addition, there is the element of luck. This goes beyond attainment. Therefore be without cruelty or injustice; if you use this way to fight, you should feel your victories to be backed by heaven.

At the beginning of every lecture Master Kien* would say, reading through large numbers of papers is not as good as spending a day learning figures. Though it seems like a diversion, when you return you find you can handle things extremely quickly. (This was published in *Gakushidan*, written by Tanaka Okura, a pupil of Master Kien.) This is the same

---

* Minagawa Kien (1735–1807): Confucian scholar, intellectual, and poet, with many connections amongst the artistic and literary worlds, such as the painter Maruyama Okyo, with whom he studied and his student Nagasawa Rosetsu. He was known as an accomplished painter and calligrapher himself. Matsuura Seizan began to study from him in 1791.

as studying swordsmanship. The swordsmanship you have learned is no better than it was before even though you have used it numbers of times without thinking. Even if you can do the movement it is not a genuine technique. Learning the meaning of the technique is the most important thing you can do. If you don't do this it will be difficult to develop real swordsmanship. In the sword, too, there is much learning. In my style there are many who do not know this.

When the people of old accompanied their lords, sword in hand, they would almost always hold the hilt. We can see this in old paintings. Everyone is doing it. Even in recent times, when I was young, in the middle of town or in the fields, I would occasionally see the followers assigned to accompany the young lord during his childhood doing this. As far as the men of old are concerned it might be said this behavior was not exclusively the preserve of swordsmanship—after all, everyone took these kinds of precautions. Even nowadays those who practice swordsmanship want to be like this. In recent years it's been impossible to see people who hold their sword like this—they have vanished.

In the *Mengzi*, in Mengzi's response to the Mohist Yi Zhi,[*] it says, in connection with seeing the abandoned corpses of your parents, "This is breaking trust. They turned away and did not look. Sweat appeared on their foreheads. Was that sweat not for the sake of others? *What was in their hearts was revealed on their faces.*" In swordsmanship, you should use a similar principle. I do not mean that it is necessary to look at the whole section about abandoned corpses, but the part that has been emphasized. The "heart" is the mind (*shin*). The "face" is the "form"(*gyo*). "Revealed" is the sword (*tou*). You must apply yourself to understand this.

---

[*] One of the followers of Mozi; Mohism was an influential school of philosophy during the Warring States period. Other than this reference, little is known of Yi Zhi.

In Qi Jiguang's *Ji Xiao Xin Shu*[*] it says, "In case of attack by pirates, a field camp should always set up braziers 20 paces apart, and each squad should burn all the wood in a single pile to keep watch over the night. If they see the pirates, they are already prepared to resist them, so the enemy cannot approach independently. Seeing what we have done, their skill fades away. *The pirates, who look from the dark into the light, become vulnerable to our attack when they advance.*" This corresponds very closely to swordsmanship. I have already added emphasis. There is no need to read beyond this. When engaging an opponent, if we are in darkness, and the enemy is placed in the light, it as if we are looking at the light from the dark. You should appreciate the flavor of this and ponder it carefully.

The master said, among victories there are some which are unexpected. When you lose, there are no inexplicable losses. He was asked what kinds of victories are inexplicable. He replied, when you follow the path of swordsmanship, it is certainly possible to win even though your spirit is not fearless. Looking back at your spirit on these occasions, you will see that this is an anomaly. When asked why there are no inexplicable defeats, he replied, if you act contrary to the way of swordsmanship, at such times there is no doubt about your defeat. On hearing this, his guest bowed down to him.

Generally, when it comes to the secrets of swordsmanship, whatever has been passed on should not to be kept hidden exactly as it was heard. Why? Because if you just keep these pristine techniques without having tested them yourself, when you use them you will find they will not bring you the victory you hoped for. No matter how precious the secret that has been passed down to you it should have been tested by the

---

[*] Qi Jiguang (1528–1588) a general of the Ming period who became famous for helping defeat incursions of pirates in the South of China. His work *Ji Xiao Xin Shu* (*A New Book of Effective Disciplines*) reflected his experiences.

master or by someone who knows it, before being made a secret. Anyone who has not once tested them has no grounds for calling them secrets.

Mengzi said, "There are times to die and times not to die. Death weakens bravery." In swordsmanship you should think about what Honshintou-ryu* (Essential or True Mind sword style) means. Warriors always aim to be brave, this is something any warrior will always say. Nevertheless, when this breaks down, the primary cause is surely doubt. And so sword technique does not push forward attacking regardless. Avoid the formidable. In all things, certainty of victory is crucial. You should strive to understand this. I have already stated the true meaning of the name Honshintou-ryu elsewhere.

In the *Opinions* of the Zen teacher, Changsha Jingcen† it says, "Though you may say 'yes, good' to those who remain unmoving while practicing the 'meditation on a hundred foot pole,' they haven't yet begun to get the real meaning. You may, by all means, walk around while 'on a hundred foot pole,' for the worlds of the ten directions are all contained within your body." This is the same as the highest concepts of swordsmanship. For beginning students this is surely difficult to understand. But if you completely understand it, it will be no different from *mu-ichi no jutsu* (without a single technique).

This may seem funny but it is primarily an allegory about the attitude of a swordsman: picture him as he stands facing a sage or a wise man, ready to cut him down with his sword; he should bring no thought into the matter. However, now take Confucius and imagine he is a master of the sword. Now this is an amusing idea: no one ever heard of him reaching the heights of swordsmanship. However, if Confucius allowed you to take up your sword and face him, even if you were completely defeated, you would still have the experience. For as long as you

---

* The style of swordsmanship studied by the founder of the Shingyoto-ryu.

† Changsha Jingcen (ca.800–868) Chinese Zen monk.

train, you would remember with pleasure what he told you. So, to take this further, in the chapter on hometown and politics from the *Analects* it is written, "When in his hometown, he spoke like someone of no ability. When he was at the ancestral mausoleum or the imperial court, he spoke straightforwardly. If he met a minor official at court he would speak openly, if he met an important official he would be restrained, and if he met the ruler, he would be respectful. He was always moderate in this." There are more things like this in his words, but all of them follow the same approach. Let's examine this.

To be like the philosopher, you should know how to be completely prepared inside and out. You should consider this carefully. Thus in terms of swordsmanship, if you were looking for an opening to somehow attack the master, you would find none. Indeed, in the end, it would undoubtedly be you who showed the opening and would be cut. The master was praised for his skill in guiding people naturally. If we look at this, this is the same situation as a swordsman who has received a certificate of mastery.

In general, when accompanying your lord, bearing his sword, carry it in your right hand as you walk. In recent times no one seems to query this. The reason for this is, in the Kyougen of Noh too, handed down traditions have plainly become accepted conventions. Accordingly, when your lord's sword is in your right hand, you carry your own in your left hand. Further, among the *Articles of Knowledge of Discipline* of the Ogasawara,* known throughout society as the teachers of etiquette, it explains the leader of a nobleman's procession should carry his sword in his right hand. The reason for the sword to be carried in the left hand is because it is convenient to draw. The leader of the procession does not wear a sword so he carries one in his right hand. Although I have heard this

---

* The Ogasawara clan was famous for its role in the codification and preservation of rules of etiquette.

about carrying a sword, when you accompany your master, it is difficult to exercise proper caution if you are carrying his sword in your right hand. If, for example someone attempted to kill your lord, would this difficulty not become the cause of disgrace? Furthermore, suppose someone were skilled in drawing with their left hand, and harbored the intention to harm his ruler what would a loyal, brave retainer do? At these times the attendants should be exercising caution entirely on their lord's behalf. The point is, first, when you are accompanying your master, bearing his sword, the hilt of your sword you're holding in your left hand should be pointing forward, the sword should be held in *suiryuu* (flowing water). *Suiryuu* means the hilt is pointing up and the sheath is pointing downwards. This is the position normally called breaking the angle (diagonal) and therefore is known as *suiryuu*. Your place is on the far left of your master. Well now, how should you exercise this caution? If is there is cause and your lord sees a chance to draw quickly, depending on the opportunity, holding it in the same position, fall back, and place yourself near your lord's left side with the hilt thrust forwards. Taking advantage of this momentum, your lord can draw the sword out easily. Though your body is particularly concerned with your lord, your energy should be completely focussed. (If you are suddenly forced to defend yourself before your lord has grasped his sword, still holding this sword, you should draw your own sword and cut down the enemy. This is why the right hand is free.)

In addition to this detailed information, there is a rule I have thought of. You should learn it. With the same caution as the men of old, Lord Sadaie's[*] hawk from the *Three Hundred Verses*,

---

[*] Fujiwara no Sadaie (also known as Fujiwara no Teika) (1162–1241): poet, critic, and editor.

The sparrowhawk, constantly changing right and left;
The man from China settled it on the right.

In the notation to the mythology it says *tadasaki* refers to
the left; *myori* is right. In the comments of Chancellor Saionji
Kintsune* it mentions that formerly hawks were flown on the
right hand. However, it also says that although flown on the
right, because of a warrior's concern for his sword, it changed
to the left about halfway through the period. Knowing this,
you should be able understand this verse. After all, in an
emergency you can draw your sword. Although hawks are
used by the major military families, their purpose is really
recreational. In traveling that's why you should be solely concerned with being vigilant. However, as a warrior, depending
on your study of the sword, you should be certain to follow
the explanation above. That's why I decided to give this somewhat detailed account.

Speed ideally comes from within calm. Therefore when
someone creates speed from force, even if it has the outward
appearance of speed, the inside is empty. You should remember the feel of this well. The swordsman should always be prepared.

These days, though there are many swordsman, all of
whom wear two swords at their side, they don't know why
this is so. If I put forward my ideas strongly, they will treat it
as so much idle talk, so I'll discuss it first in concrete terms.
The reason that warriors bear swords is not on account of their
virtue—at first, no one carried swords as a matter of course.
Then, as a precaution, they began to carry them. From there,
they eventually took to wearing two swords. This was in times
that were extremely troubled; in more peaceful times they
did not do so. But, because people don't know about peaceful

---

* Saionji Kintsune (1171–1244): a powerful member of the court and friend
of Fujiwara Sadaie.

and troubled times, they just follow the old customs without considering the alternative. In today's society, if they follow a particular path of study, for example, and are aware of its significance, this does not mean they should just follow the custom indiscriminately. Recently I was looking through a work called *Wakun-no-Shiori*[*] edited by Tanigawa Kotosuga.[†] It said that under the monarchical system the amassing of weapons by disbanded soldiers was not allowed. (Joseishi said that by weapons it means spears and swords. The ancient Imperial Court layed down the regulations that swords were not to be worn. Those in official positions were to be armed). After the Onin Civil War,[‡] everything was in chaos. (Joseishi notes Onin was during the just rule of the Ashikaga Shogunate, 346 years ago).

In the *Kaitoushokoku-ki* which mentions customs of the Muromachi period, an edict was received, stating everyone was required to wear a single sword. (Joseishi: the *Kaitoushokoku-ki* was written by a Korean author named Sin Suk Chu.[§] The preface is dated 1471. This year would be our Bunmei 3, five years after Onin. At around this time all warriors, including lords, customarily wore one sword). In a painting of an artisan's poetry meeting it is the same. (Joseishi notes this painting by the ancestor of the Tosa School, Mitsunobu,[¶] depicts various aspects of the life of artisans. In these pictures, the people of those times all wear only one sword, so the proof is not only from foreign sources. We can see Mitsunobu

---

[*] *A Guide to Japanese Readings*: an early dictionary.

[†] Tanigawa Kotosuga (1709–1776): a kokugaku scholar and friend of the younger Motoori Norinaga (see above).

[‡] Onin Civil War (1467–1477): a wasteful war that laid waste to the capital, Kyoto, and marked the start of the Sengoku period.

[§] Sin Suk Chu (1417–1475): Korean Confucian scholar and government official, credited with invention of hangul; also took part in diplomatic missions to Japan and China.

[¶] Tosa Mitsunobu (1434–1525): Japanese painter who founded the Tosa School. Held several important positions related to painting.

mentioned in the *History of Painting* (*Honcho Gashi**—1698).
In Meiou 7 (1498) he was appointed to the Ministry of Justice,
5th Rank. This was some 317 years ago, in the time of Shogun
Ashikaga Yoshizumi). Nowadays among performers of the
Kyougen that's associated with Noh, those who accompany the
master follow on behind, bearing a *chutou*. (This is thought
to be a long sword, which is the same thing as a *tachi*. What
is nowadays called a *wakizashi* is called a "sword"—*tou*.) So
presently (which is to say the time the author is writing) warriors should be aware that people wore two swords because
they were "followers" or in case of emergencies in the "world
of a thousand halberds." (Joseishi: "follower" is a literary term,
which is used because they follow in someone's footsteps.
They are people who walk behind their lord. In other words,
we would say a vassal in someone's retinue. If it was now the
sword carried would be a *tachi*. The term "world of a thousand
halberds" refers to times when battles were common.) In the
laws and ordinances of Tenwa 2 (1683), the *Henesho no Hai*†
states "The wearing of two swords is prohibited." (Joseishi:
Tenwa 2 was during the early years of Shogun Mitsuyoshi,
when the laws and ordinances were announced. From this
we can see that until then, farmers, artisans, and townspeople
wore two swords as they wanted. We would now call these two
swords *daisho*—long and short.) This also shows that previously warriors did not wear two swords. In fact nobody wore
swords. All the people of those times have passed away and
are nothing but corpses. So you carry swords as a precaution
when you accompany people of higher standing, your father,
or men of learning. Furthermore, you should be armed as a
precaution on your own behalf. So those who know only that
it is a warrior's prerogative to wear swords, are just those who
make a livelihood out of swordsmanship. In society, with the

---

* *History of Painting in this Realm.*
† *Records of Artisans.*

help of cosmetics, there are many who mimic actors' voices. Women and children find them hilarious. This is because they know the person being mimicked. If you make a mental comparison, it will be amusing. But swordsmen, too, in normal practice merely fantasize about duels with real swords. Why, oh why?

In the past, once I heard someone say you should think of *kyo-jitsu* in terms of the opening and closing of doors or sliding screens. This is because the kind of person who throws them open and slams them shut is someone who is empty inside. However fast they go in and out, someone who opens and closes them carefully is full inside, he said. Accordingly I made up my mind to follow this injunction. Beyond that, I understood little of its benefit. Having reached my last years, thinking about this I see it has increasingly become an everyday part of my swordsmanship. I put this here as something I hope people will think about.

In Mengzi's *Gong Sun Chou* there is a discussion of archery, "The superior man draws the bow but doesn't release. It is as if it has already leapt to the target." You should compare this to the way of the sword. The reason for this is that even when engaged in a match, when you attack you should never think about the opponent's appearance and ability. Just start straight away. When you proceed in this way, all the opportunities to strike the opponent arise from you yourself. Josuiken, in contests with other schools, always drew his sword and advanced. Because you have adopted no posture, you are ready to strike the opponent immediately. Zesuiken said, consequently, you have already won. This is how the archery of which Mengzi speaks corresponds to the sword.

"People should have a wide range of knowledge. If not they will undoubtedly be defeated in the military arts." This comes from the *Ji Xiao Xin Shu* (this was written by a general of the Ming period, Qi Jiguang, a soldier through and through—

you should take his eyewitness accounts of the battlefield as accurate). It also says, "Normally in battle formations when 100,000 men advance in formation, the brave can't forge ahead, the timid can't retreat, the spears are clumped together, some will be slain, some flee, abandoning their swords they will pray, abandoning themselves to death they will be slain. Others only advance in a huddle. It is almost impossible to move their arms." This is something you should be aware of. A swordsman fights a single opponent with the intention of using precise techniques; a chase must be very different. This is something you have to think about seriously.

In *Mengzi* it says, "A chariot maker may give a man a rule and measure but cannot make him skilled in them." Nowadays, the same applies to swordsmanship. If you take up a wooden sword in a basic technique, or make a distinction when using a bamboo sword, this is using a "rule and measure." But a contest or real combat rests on skill. Therefore even though they are taught the "rule and measure" by their shishou (the term given to a teacher of swordsmanship) students must strive to discover the advantages and disadvantages in a contest or real combat for themselves. If not, they will not achieve mastery.

In a work called the *Wuli Xiaoshi** (Compiled by Fang Yi Zhi in the Ming Dynasty) there is mention of something called hometown sword feats. It seems to be like juggling. In this section in the *Lizi* (the name of a book) it says, "The juggler handled seven swords, he transferred them while leaping; five swords were always in the air. The master was surprised and thought it was wonderful. This is just acquired skill. It is not real technique." It is written there are still people like this. "Handle" means throw in a curve. "Transfer" is referred to in the notes as *koutetsu* which means to pass from hand to hand. "In the air" means that as they are released from the hand,

---

* *Wuli Xiaoshi (A Small Study of Things and their Principles)* (1664): an encyclopedia compiled by the scholar Fang Yi Zhi (1611–1671).

they are in the air. So because there are seven swords, two are held in the hands at any one time, five are not being held, in a continuous rotation. It is certainly an unusual skill. That's why the master thought it was wonderful. But it is only an acquired skill. Fang Yi Zhi said it was not true technique. With regard to this piece, this is something swordsmen should be able to see. With acquired skill, if you practice, you will be able to pick up the tempo easily. From the comment that this is not true technique it is clear there were people in Ming China who had a good understanding of swordsmanship. The principle embodied in an art is, in short, the intention of following a way. In the case of swordsmanship, of course there is a way, too. People have their natural way of doing things, but for an art or a way, after all, it should be practiced as described above; as far as swordsmanship goes the most direct path, straight as a bullet, is repeatedly wielding the sword. You could say this is the way to victory. I have written about this theory of swordsmanship elsewhere. People reading this should examine this theory and path carefully.

In the *Bugei Shoden*,[*] it tells of a man called *Tsukahara Bokuden*.[†] (Bokuden lived during the Tenshou Period 1573-1592; his skill in the sword resounded through the country). Once, when travelling on a ferryboat in Koushu, Yabase in Omi, he gave a criticism of swordsmanship. In summary what he said was, "I too have practiced swordsmanship since my youth, engaging with the typical vigor of my age. Now I have let go of thinking about how to secure victory, instead planning how not to lose." He said nothing more of the matter. A man listening to him thought he was just a kindly old priest. When he asked what school of strategy he belonged to,

---

[*] *Honcho Bugei Shoden* (1714) by Hinatsu Shigetaka contains brief biographies of over a hundred masters of different martial arts including swordsmanship, the spear, archery, and ju-jutsu.

[†] Tsukahara Bokuden (1489–1571): a famous swordsman who founded the Kashima Shinto-ryu.

he replied, "Well, it's just the school of not losing and winning without fighting." The man said, "If it's the school of winning without fighting, why do you wear those two swords at your waist?" Bokuden listened and said, "What was passed down directly to me was that the two swords are to cut down the shoots of evil thoughts." On hearing this the man said, "Let's have a contest and see if you can win through not fighting." Bokuden replied, "Though certainly the sword of my mind is a life giving sword, if my opponent is an evil man, it becomes a mere killing sword." For a commonplace swordsman of that time, this would be seen as tantamount to cowardice, but it is said that lightning doesn't strike from a clear sky, and this story has been passed on. It is right that Bokuden is renowned. I think that those who talk about the sword should savor this principle.

People involved in the arts of the warrior often see stories from the Noh plays and the like without getting much out of them. First, lets look at the chant from the play *Ebira** from the point of view of the swordsman:

> The enemy warriors see me,
> They cheer! What adversaries,
> Don't let them escape, they say.
> I am in the middle of eight riders;
> My helmet is struck off:
> My hair hangs down like a boy's.
> Three of my retainers mounted,
> Arrayed behind me.
> I cut the man facing me straight down,†
> And turning again to meet the attack,
> I use the wheel cut.

---

* A famous Noh drama featuring the ghost of Kajiwara Genta Kagesue who retells his exploits in the battle of Ikuta. The play is named for the quiver (*ebira*) in which Genta carries a branch of plum blossoms.

† This overhead strike is called *ogamiuchi*.

What do you think of this? Do you think it's just fine words? It was not actually written during the period of the Heike War,[*] but Noh plays were generally composed from around the middle of the Ashikaga period. Even though this battle scene, which tells of Genta in the middle of a sword fight is not from this period, the writer would have been familiar with these situations. First, the eight riders. These are eight mounted warriors of the Heike clan. Genta has as allies three retainers, making a total of four men. So "in the middle of eight riders" means the four of them were surrounded by eight men. You should realize that is because this battleground was a flat area of open fields. They would be positioned as in the diagrams. These should stir the interest of swordsmen. What do you make of them?

Fig 1.[†]

Surrounded, whichever way they turn, front and back, left and right, the situation is difficult. With the associated retainers arrayed behind, the situation would look like this.

---

[*] Usually known as the Gempei War (1180–1185), it was fought between the Minamoto (Genji) and Taira (Heike) clans. The Minamoto emerged victorious to found the Minamoto shogunate and begin the period of warrior ascendancy. It forms the backdrop to a number of well-known Noh plays.

[†] The characters read: center right, Genta; center left, retainer; surrounding characters, opponent.

Fig 2.*

If we look at this, surrounded by enemies in all directions, although their number is half that of their assailants, they can deal with attacks from all four directions.

So he cut down the enemy with *ogamiuchi*—this is *setsu-kofu-tou* from the Eight Transmitted Swords.† It is just such a technique that must have been passed down as one of the "Six types of Swords." (Nothing more is said of the theory of *ogamiuchi*).

> And turning again to meet the attack,
> I use the wheel cut.

Among the Eight Transmitted Swords is *sasentou-usentou*: "cut left and right." If you have been taught this, you will, of course, be aware that this was originally a mounted technique. First, this is the general meaning. If you take other examples and reflect on them using this as your base, you can understand the motivation of people in the past.

In Tang China, on Mount Niu-Tou, lived the Zen teacher Fa Jung,‡ who gave this reply to Bo Luwang:

---

* The characters read: bottom position, Genta; other three positions, retainer.

† A group of sword techniques still practiced in the Shingyoto-ryu.

‡ Fa Jung (594-697) founder of the Ox-head school of Zen Buddhism based on Mount Niu Tou (Ox-head Mountain).

If you desire to know the original mind
It is like a returning to a dream.

Swordsmen can probably appreciate the significance of these words. The reason is that with regard to the original mind, once you have determined that winning is dependent on the mind, you will achieve a state where it seems, after all, to be a trifling matter. The state of achieving victory is just to bring out the single mind. In fact it is as if you are within a dream. The state that you want is where form and technique are one. (Fa Jung's commentary may be seen in the *Goto Wu Teng Hui Yuan.**)

One day as I was looking through *An Outline of Medical Plants* (a work that deals with the materials that are used in medical treatments, and relating successful cures), and found that among the materials the physician brought up there was an entry for swords. "In the case of ingesting poison from snakes or insects, take two swords, grind them together, add water and drink the resulting liquid. In the case of an insect becoming lodged in your ear, take two swords, scrape them together next to the ear to make a noise and it will come out of its own accord. The liquid made from rubbing swords is also of some minor benefit in cases of discharge." For "hemorrhoids, piles, or anal prolapse, or cases of extrusion, or where there is unbearable earache," I saw that you could smear some of it on. The sheath was also mentioned. "To treat a sudden sharp pain known as a devil's blow, take one which is 23-inches in length and use it to apply water to the sore point." I saw that if these were the swords that were normally worn, it was all the better. However this has absolutely nothing to do with swordsmanship, and it's not the sort of thing that warriors are expected to know. I am writing it down with some reluctance.

---

* *Goto's Collected Essentials of the Five Lamps (1252).*

It seems he was only something like a doctor: the liquid made from grinding two swords refers to the liquid from sharpening and polishing. (The liquid from sharpening razors would be fine.) "Hemorrhoids" is the same as piles. "Extrusion" refers to the condition in women when, after giving birth, the womb protrudes from the genitalia, and which can, it said, be restored to its original condition. In short, the liquid from polishing has a closing or retracting effect. What is referred to as devil's blow and is also known as devil's strike is so named for the following reason: it refers to cases of sudden illness when you unexpectedly feel pains over the whole body as if you are being stabbed; it feels like your body has been run through: the pain is excruciating—it's as if you are in hell. For myself, though there were no detailed accounts of successful treatments, this is part of broad knowledge on the topic of the sword. Let me explain. The basis of swordsmanship is killing and defeating your enemies, but this may be little different from the actions of robbers and violent thugs. However, if you use it in times of emergency, when accompanying your teacher or father, this violence can save you. Therefore cutting someone down when you are in a dire situation allows you to proceed in safety. If you have this kind of outlook it is a virtuous art. And so from times past, if people like this have been admired, should not all the various branches of sword use be considered benevolent, seeing as they provided quick aid, sword in hand, or at least have the potential of doing so. This should give you a smile.

While I was looking through Minagawa Kien's marginal notations to *The Customs of Zhou*, there was an account of a dance instructor which I will recount briefly:

I was pondering on Shejing (of the Ming Dynasty, who went on to serve under the Manchus) who said, "Dance is one branch of etiquette and music. The late king repeatedly said, 'Dance works the muscles and bones, regulates the blood vessels engages the limbs softly and in co-ordination; it compares favorably to exercise in terms of deportment and to walking and running in terms of enjoyment.'" I borrowed the *Dances of the State of Wu*,* and thus I saw the similarities with the military preparations that I have learned. However, the dancing of old was not, of course, practiced for recreation, but for teaching correct use of the body and mind. Thus, those skilled with the sword today, be they from illustrious families or famous in their own right, even though they may not have penetrated the mysteries of the spirit of swordsmanship, must not think to make light of it, but should also take care to preserve the aspects related to the maintenance of good health.

In Senryu-ji Temple, in Izumimura, Tama County, Bishu (the present-day Setagaya) you can obtain a charm against smallpox. It is extremely effective. And so it was, if any of my childhood friends showed symptoms, they would be sure to have this form of self-protection, and incidences of the disease, and indeed its seriousness, fell greatly, and there were no fatalities. Consequently I had a strong faith in its efficacy. However, one year there was a child who developed a hereditary illness and whose head was covered in scabs, which would sometimes weep. The doctor said, if this is indeed smallpox, death is inevitable. I secretly got a charm from the temple on his behalf and prostrated myself according to its injunctions. Never before had I been so desperate. There are similar diseases of varying degrees of seriousness, but this could cure them all. Consequently I felt increasingly that this child would be safe. However as the disease continued, it became serious. In the evening, I saw the symptoms. It was as the doctor had said. The disease took hold and finally he died.

I also knew someone who had been brought up as a sumo wrestler. One particular year there was a ten-day public tour-

---

* These were dances that included both a military and civilian element.

nament in the grounds of Nishikubo Hachiman Shrine. He was invited to go. On coming to see him off, I told him he must not lose. Accordingly I gave him *katsuobushi** as a spur to success. Even so, he lost on the first day. I wasn't worried. I didn't feel ashamed of him, he had always had an indomitable spirit and in front of his residence in Araimachi there was a sacred statue of Fudo, in front of which he would pray. People who did this received *utsurukage*—divine aid. Having done so he felt relieved; more than that, he believed. Even so, on the second day, he lost again. When I consider these incidents, it is not saying there is no spirit of Fudo, nor does it mean the amulet of Senryu-ji was unproven. Simply put, people should be strong rather than rely on divine protection. If you are possessed by a spirit, you have already received that benefit if you are mentally strong, as if it were divine aid. Making our minds resolute is nothing more than this. With your whole body unified, you should purify the six gates of perception.

Those people who admire the *iai* of our school show a strange fixation for what various other schools term *iai*. The reason I say this is that *iai* is like a literary term—it is not drawing the sword. When you match *i* (being or presence) with an opponent (the word *au* means the spirit of opposition), depending on the mental attitude, it is called "projecting the spirit to give victory." I will tell you the key to learning this: the potential of drawing the sword and cutting down the opponent is present while the sword is still sheathed. Even as you glimpse an opportunity as the opponent moves, that cut is already present in the sheathed sword (*saya no uchi*). It is this spirit I teach. But at times you may hear praise for the sword drawing of the Jikishinkage-ryu too—this is because of *saya no uchi*. Although we are not particularly concerned with the immature preference shown by some schools, in our

---

* Dried flaked bonito is symbolic of victory. The first two syllables (*katsu*) are pronounced the same way as "victory."

school there are actually two scrolls among the *mokuroku* concerned with this technique. In the preface it states, "This is the technique of *iai*: although there is a range at which you may draw the sword and attack, the essence of this is controlling the enemy without drawing your sword. Adapting to the moment is mysterious and 'divine.'" However this is no common transmission; and it is no common technique. If you have not actually cultivated this ability, it will be hard to understand. Nonetheless, you should grasp the essence of these words.

When I was young and put great energy into this art, for the sake of matches I put great efforts into strengthening my wrists. It was around this time, when I had not yet started my studies under Master Kien, on my journey east, I was evaluating everyone in Naniwa, one by one. One year, on the journey to Fushimi, Master Kien and I were on the same ship. While he was talking I interrupted, "For the art of the sword, surely one needs great strength. Now looking at you, Master, even though you wear two swords at your waist, you are probably not prepared to use them. So if you are not ready to make use of your blade for killing, if you were to be attacked just at this moment, what sort of art would you use?"

"In answer, sir, from what you said it appears you have no understanding at all. Even though it may not at first seem to be the case, when I take up my swords, I never fail to steel my resolve. If what you say is true, you should cut me down right now. I am willing to reveal that resolve now. However, if it is not as you said, and you decline, your words are false. If so, you may say it is on account of this art, this technique, that you have given me no concern." When I heard this, I understood for the first time the unity of Master Kien's moral principles and understood the true heart of the art of the sword. Trusting that it was as the master had said, my threats did not affect him. If I could not draw, I certainly did not have the skill to cut him. Which is to say, Master Kien had intimidated me. Moreover, in the way he regarded me, there was no slight. He believed from the start that Heaven's way lay in making me unable to perform acts of injustice such as killing. This decision was truly the pure spirit of the sword. This recounts the situation just as it happened.

If, from the three schools of thought, we take Buddhism, although they follow the path of the Buddha and humble themselves before saints of long ago, the sects have become increasingly separate from their distant origins. Accordingly each master points to the mystery with a different finger, and every garden is built on mutual contradictions. Let's compare this saying to the ideas of swordsmen. Nowadays all the various styles are like this. If you were to adhere to this approach you would be unable to understand even a single technique. Perhaps an understanding of the real nature of victory and defeat is contained within this example.

It was said that in the domain of Hirado there was a style of two sword use. This originally came from Miyamoto Musashi, and the school is called the Enmei-ryu. I did not study this school and I don't know anything about its principles, but while I was looking through a discourse on Buddhism recently, in a teaching attached to a sutra it said:

Shingetsu no enmei naru wo mizu to.
The clear circle of the new moon reflected in the water.

Is the school named after this *enmei* (clear circle)?[*] Did this "clear circle of the new moon" encapsulate the main point of this school's spirit of the sword or did they just take the name from elsewhere?

---

[*] *Shingetsu* is written as "mind-moon" and so *shingetsu no enmei* also means "perfection of the mind."

This was taken out from a well-known collection of stories. Huan Wen* married the daughter of Mingdi, Princess
Nan-kang. Wen, after a campaign of pacification, took Emperor Li Shi's younger sister as concubine. He favored her
greatly, always spending time with her and later living with
her. Princess Nan-kang heard of this, and with some dozens
of maids, came and drew her blade to attack her. Lady Li's
head deserved combs, but even with her hair hanging down
to the floor, she cut an elegant figure. Gradually sinking to the
ground, her fingers which were binding her hair stiffened and
she turned to face the princess saying, "My kingdom is de-
stroyed, my family slain. I was brought here against my will. It
is all one to me whether I die this day or live for years to come.
I have said my farewells and accept my sorry fate." On hearing
this the princess laid aside her sword, and stepping forward
to embrace her she said, "Even I feel pity now I see you. How
much more must that old rogue." In the end they saw much
of each other.

Once, when reading this, someone doubted it saying,
"Earlier it said she drew her blade, but later it says she laid her
sword aside. The two do not match up. The first statement,
that she drew her blade is probably a mistake." Accordingly I
checked it and pointed out that this kind of thing must be
seen as literary style, from which we should infer the real situation. This is the spirit of swordsmanship. In this case, taking
"blade" as the edge of the sword, in the *Yupian*† it says "sword"
is "blade."

In the commentaries, "sword" can also mean "soldier." If
you look at old characters, this comment says they imitate the
back of the sword and the blade, which is why the character
for a "sword's blade" is written incorporating the character

---

for sword. Again, "*nuku*" according to the commentaries can mean "select" as well as "draw." In comments on etiquette, "*nuku*" is mentioned as having the additional meaning, "fast." Nowadays we would say "pfft" or "pull out with a swoosh." "Draw a blade" could be taken as "draw out an edged weapon—pfft!" Princess Nan-kang, filled with hate and anger towards Li's sister pulled out her sword and advanced upon her. That is why it is written, "*ha wo nuku*"—drew her blade. Later it is written that she laid her sword aside—as before the commentaries say "sword" means "soldier," and is just the name given to a tool that cuts, and so it is this object's name. So, when Princess Nan-kang goes forward angrily, and upon seeing Lady Li's bearing, her mature grace, realizing this tool is something she doesn't need, she throws it away. "Lay aside" in the correct tone can mean "discard." In the *History of the Jin Dynasty* it is written, "The Princess laid it on the ground as a test." If she had wanted to do that, she should have used a stern voice. If we look at what it said, the reason it uses "throw down," when Princess Nan-kang notes the misery of Lady Li, is that she throws down the implement she is holding so she can quickly go to embrace her. Therefore in the passage it says, "She went forward and embraced her." You should know how to distinguish between these two ways of reading the characters. Which is to say, if you know how to make this distinction you will have the kind of keen eye that allows you to see into the nature of people such as swordsmen. (According to the *Shishuo Xinyu*,[*] at first Lady Li did not hear the princess. By the time she did, she was already there accompanied by dozens of maids. She drew a naked blade and advanced. Afterwards there is no mention of laying down her sword. If we take "naked" to mean "bright" as in "naked sunlight"

---

[*] A collection of literary and historical anecdotes written by Liu Yiqing in the first half of the 5th century.

and the "naked day," "draw a naked blade" becomes a phrase meaning a highly polished blade, which reflects the splendid nature of its owner. Again, in the commentaries to *Shishuo Xinyu*, in the account it says the princess was fiercely jealous. Up until that point we are not aware, but afterwards we find out; accordingly the princess pays a visit to Lady Li, her sword drawn. Thereupon, seeing her filled with longing, the princess was so affected she threw away her sword, went forward, and embraced her, saying "My dear, when I saw you I was again filled with pity.") Here, too, "drawing her blade she strode forward," because it is written to convey a particular thought, "blade" is used. Afterwards, because it is just a tool that she discards, it is written as "sword." You should examine this to understand the underlying spirit.

On one occasion, my teacher was sitting with Lord Matsudaira Zushyu.* In the course of conversation, Zushyu mentioned Noh and said that, in Komparu Noh, when an actor points at something, the left side of his body comes forward and right pulls back, and his eyes stare as he gestures, allowing us to really feel that he is pointing at something. If, for example the actor points to a cryptomeria tree at the side of the stage just as he has learnt, in time with the lyrics of the song as they say, "Yonder cryptomeria," but without really feeling the tree is there, anything he points to will be flat. Even if he chants "cryptomeria" for all he's worth, there will be no tree. Therefore if he is indicating a tree or any pretend object this is important. So he must create a cryptomeria in his mind, imagine that is the tree he is pointing at, and when he points at that tree with his fan he must have the sensation of that image before his eyes. That is why it gives the appearance of reality. For normal people who have just learned the dance as it

---

* Lord Matsudaira Zushyu: Zushyu was a title: Lord of Izu, which refers to the origins of this branch (the Okochi) of the large Matsudaira clan. In this case, probably Matsudaira Nobuteru (1660–1725).

is, there will be no such intention—no matter how much you point at the cryptomeria in the wings, if you don't see the image in your mind, you will just be waving your fan around. You should discriminate between these two approaches.

The master responded naturally to his neighbor, but if you go away and think about it, you can apply this spirit in learning swordsmanship, too. For example, when you are practicing techniques and you raise your sword to strike at the opponent's shoulder, fixing your mind solely on cutting with a single stroke, if you strike with this sword it will cut truly. However, if you just go through the motions you have learned as you strike, although the movement of the cut will be the same, it will fall spectacularly short of your expectations.

You should be aware that this is a part of all styles of swordsmanship. Indeed, Zushyu's comment is exceptionally astute.

Let's take a look and see whether swordsmanship was present in early China. In the Ming period, in the *Wuli Xiaoshi*, it speaks of the history of swordsmanship, relating the tale of Ganjiang and Moye, man and wife, who were martyred for their work. (Long ago this story was of the swords Ganjiang and Moye. Moreover, one of these swords turned into a dragon at a place called Yanpingjin. To me this just jumps out as fiction. It has nothing to do with swordsmanship. Therefore I will say nothing more of it here.) With Lai Tan's* "Night Tempered," we enter the mysterious world of *mukei*—formlessness. (This is in the *Liezi* and refers to Lai Tan, who had a sword called "Night Tempered." It is said this spirit sword was unlike other swords of the world. As it had this quality of the mysterious, it has nothing to do with the swordsmanship of today, and therefore I will omit it.) What

---

* Lai Tan: this story is told in Book 5 of the *Liezi*. Lai Tan was seeking revenge for the death of his father and borrowed a sword that passed through its targets, leaving no mark or wound.

is called swordsmanship with reference to Lu Goujian[*] is just what one would think it would be. (This is essentially what is related in the *Shiji*[†] after Jinke[‡] failed to stab Huangdi, a man named Goujian was discussing swordsmanship. According to the *Shiji*, when he heard the attempt on Huangdi had failed, he said to himself, "What a shame. I regret now that I did not discuss the arts of swordsmanship with him. How little I understand men. That this should have happened!" The compiler of the *Wuli Xiaoshi*, Fang Yizhi, wrote the conversations as he imagined them to have been, but is the *Shiji* not filled with such conversations? In the previous section, Jinke, he writes as he pleases about attacking with a sword. In the commentaries to the *Lushi*[§] it speaks of sword techniques: "Holding a short sword, penetrate deeply, be able to move in any direction in an instant," so you should also be aware of this as a type of swordsmanship. You should look at the connected piece that follows. However, we cannot really know what it was that Fang Yizhi was trying to point out. Stories include much that is strange and deceiving and which can no longer be seen. (This means that there are many stories that mention swordsmanship, but they are all strange, mysterious, deluded, and odd. Now that they have died out, these arts, whatever they may have been, are no longer to be seen. Again, this has nothing to do with swordsmanship. However, maybe the practitioners of the strange and the odd really did possess some kind of skill.)

"In the year of the Boar (referring to the reign of the last

---

[*] Lu Goujian: little more is known of him than is mentioned in the text—apparently a famous swordsman and also an expert in *liubo*, a precursor of xiangqi or chinese chess.

[†] *Records of the Grand Historian*: compiled by Sima Qian (see above).

[‡] Assassin who attempted to kill Qin Shi Huangdi (259–210 BCE), the first Qin emperor of China (not to be confused with Huang-di, the Yellow Emperor).

[§] *The Spring and Autumn Annals of Lu.*

Ming emperor Sizong who ruled during the Kanei Period),
in a place called Zhongdu a swordsman cut off the head of
a certain detention guard, Zhang, who had treated the poor
cruelly. The event was announced on signs ten days previously, and it took place just as it had been said. At this time
the commander of Jun was Yang Yipeng. He had not sought
this. 'Aah, don't prolong the gloom of suffering,' he wrote, 'or
more, your courage will fail.'" The section in the *Wuli Xiaoshi*
goes this far. The year of the Boar occurred during the reign
of the last Ming emperor Chongzhen (Sizong), who occupied
the throne during the Kanei Period (1624-1644). In a place
called Zhongdu, there was a certain Zhang, a detention guard,
who profiteered from the poor and because he treated people
cruelly, his wickedness was well-known. However, someone
well-versed in swordsmanship managed to cut off this official
Zhang's head and escaped before anyone knew what was hap-
pening. This was probably going too far. Even so, it was said
that before his head was struck off, placards were set up tell-
ing people that within ten days Zhang will lose his head. And
so it happened: without anyone knowing how, he lost his life.
And so Yang Yipeng, commander of a place called Jun said,
"I didn't wish for this, but if there's one direction you fail to
look in, that's where it will happen." In the 11th chapter, be-
low where it says "Aah, don't prolong the gloom of suffering,"
it goes on to say, "If you don't want your energy to bend or
waver, pay attention to what is written here about appearance
and feeling. In order not to go pale you should eat and drink
something." You should think about things like this and ponder on them. As the one concerned, and all the bystanders,
were aware of the placards that had been put out earlier de-
claring Zhang would lose his head within ten days, the deed
had to be done with extreme care as a matter of course. Even
so, the kind of cut used in a case like this could never be done
without extreme speed. (This is the first point.) In the previ-

ously mentioned *Shiji* it is as the *Lushi* said, it is absolutely vital for someone with a short weapon to penetrate deeply, to move in and out freely, with great speed and agility. However, though this might not be morally praiseworthy, swift technique is not limited to this type of incident. It should be used to mysterious effect in swordsmanship. (This is the second point.) Besides, "Don't prolong the gloom of suffering," it says "or more, your courage will fail." You should be perfectly aware that if swordsmanship is to be used to achieve victory and to be of any use for your country too, it is vital that this technique be fast if it is to be praised for its service to justice. (This is the third point.)

While in service, in an antechamber or some such, when a samurai who is doing something like writing is summoned for some reason, very often the person coming answers and throws down their writing brush. This sound can be heard clearly from outside. In my opinion, people who do this are in a state of hurry: in reality this is *kyo* or unpreparedness. In swordsmanship, we would say these unprepared people's calmness is hindered. If you ask how I can say so, when they are called, they should simply respond and when they stand they should place their brush down quietly, without making a sound. If you pay strict attention to these words you should achieve the calm mind of the sword. Is this not something that beginners should know?

In selections of the music of Ying (the capital of Chu), scraps of the old writing of chants, survive, though the entirety probably will not be found. "The hips are low like a rock, while the upper body is like a green willow, the face is no different from normal, the eyes do not glance about and neck is held straight; though you chant countless times you must preserve this appearance." Although swordsmanship is not as rigid as singing, if you think hard about this concept, the sword should possess this spirit at the decisive moment in a clash with the enemy. Verse and the sword may be different as heaven and earth, but when you have achieved this calmness, they do not differ. You should take this and reflect on it. (Again, you should always be thinking about putting things to appropriate use in a contest. You should think about this very carefully.)

Ge Hanxi* of the Qing (Ge was his family name, Shouzhi his personal name, and Hanxi his courtesy name), wrote a book called *Holding the Writing Brush*, (this is a work on calligraphy explaining how to hold the brush), in which the art of writing is connected to archery.

"In manners your inner resolve must be correct: adjust your body, so afterwards you can take up the bow and arrows resolutely. When you take up the bow with determination, you have already begun your shot. This depends on your sincerity, but if your mind is correct, your brush will be correct—in effect there is no situation in which you will not be able to make use of this correctness. Therefore, people who are starting to learn calligraphy, first learn how to hold the brush." You should study this well. Again, perhaps this is related to the sword. If it is said first you learn to hold the brush, then in the art of the sword, it is equivalent to the *kamae* with the long sword. "There is no situation in which you will not be able to make use of this correctness" would be, in the case of the sword, whatever techniques you use, there is nothing which will not work effectively. "You have already started to shoot" could be stated as, similarly to the above, "is no different from striking," and "in sharpening, you are already cutting." Repeatedly "taste" these words with the sense of investigating the art of the sword.

In the 5th month of the year of the Ox (1817), Master Hayashi† (Rector of the Shogunate College) paid a visit to

---

* Ge Shouzhi (1720–1786) was the author of several works on calligraphy. *Poubitu (Holding the Writing Brush)* was published in Japan in 1809.

† Hayashi Jussai (1768–1841): neo-Confucian scholar and hereditary head (*Daigaku no kami*) of the Shogunate Yushima Seidou (Shouheikou) Confucian Academy.

Boudo and at the height of conversation, I got out one or two wooden bows to show him. Master Hayashi said that warriors of old possessed subtleties of archery that were without a doubt different from those of today. All of them had developed the spirit necessary for hitting distant targets and shooting at extreme ranges. Nowadays, the Emishi* can down a flying bird using a round wooden bow. They always hit what they shoot at. In the past they certainly would not have missed. Again, this required a strong spirit. If we take these words and apply them to swordsmanship, when facing the enemy the tip of the sword can extend far, and if you refine your spirit, your blade can crush an enemy's sword, for example. All those who do this undoubtedly believe in the use of the spirit derived from training. Knowing this energy exists look for it yourself.

Generally, people who use swordsmanship, being on the whole ill-educated, take one school and compare it to others; beginners also tend to think about which is better. This is without having an overall understanding. Whatever school it is, they share a common origin. Actually, there are no superior points. The only thing that is superior is the winner had stronger energy. In the book titled *The Two or Three Later Chronicles* (This book has not been checked in detail by the editor. It is thought to be the widely mentioned work by Tada Yoritoshi)† it says, both Jimmu Mikado‡ and Amenotomi-no-Mikoto,§ are descendants of Omi-no-Futotama-no-mikoto.¶ There was a memorial held for this ancestor, for which war-

---

* An ethnic group that lived in northeastern Japan and resisted the advance of the Yamato peoples until the 10th century. Famous for their skills as archers and riders.

† This comment appears in the text. Tada Yoritoshi (1698–1750) was a koku-gaku scholar.

‡ Jimmu Mikado: the first human emperor of Japan.

§ Amenotomi-no-Mikoto chief priest of the Imbe clan and important retainer of Jimmu.

¶ Omi-Futotama-no–mikoto: probably Ame-no Futotama-no-mikoto, legendary ancestor of the Imbe Clan.

riors, soldiers, and artisans worked together, leaving their families to take on a public role. The present day Shinto-ryu school of swordsmanship was included among these. The warriors' code comes from this. It has been passed on since ancient times. The Kashima-ryu* and Kage-ryu traditions of swordsmanship are two more related styles. (In the book the transmitted principles are mistakes. Probably the text is not genuine). Observers should be aware of this. However the Shingyoto-ryu is the tip of the Kashima-ryu. The Yagyu-ryu, Kage-ryu, Shinkage-ryu, and Jikishinkage-ryu too, are all the same style. Due to their ignorance many think that their school is special. After all, this clearly shows they lack knowledge of the principles of combat.

Sometime in the Genroku era (1688-1704), a Confucian scholar named Otaka Toshiaki wrote the preface to *Itto Ryu Kenjutsu Sho*,† in which the student of the sword desires to achieve a state of *mushin*. "They don't simply rely on predicting what is about to happen; they don't over-estimate. They are bold and possess the spirit of the true mind. Students who have this, are as one inside and out, theory and technique simultaneously become clear, there should be no partiality; the traces of victory and defeat appear clearly in the gap between taking and losing the initiative, between give and take. However, taking and losing initiative is a matter of sensing; giving and taking is a matter of energy. Both sensing and energy derive from the *kokoro*. Energy strives to be like unwavering courage; sensing strives to be like an undimmed light; the *kokoro* strives, in its emptiness, to respond to changing circumstances without hesitation. If you are indeed truly like

---

* Kashima-ryu, Yagyu-ryu, Kage-ryu, Shinkage-ryu and Jikishinkage-ryu: famous schools of swordsmanship. The Yagyu-ryu, Shinkage-ryu and Jikishinkage-ryu are all directly descended from the Kage-ryu. The founder of the Kage-ryu had connections with the Kashima-ryu.

† This may refer to the well-known work on the Itto-ryu, *Ittosai Sensei Kenpo Sho (Notes on Master Ittosai's Swordsmanship)*(1664) by Kotoda Toshisada.

this, in advance and retreat none will dare strike you, moving left and right, none will bar your way. Advance and retreat, left and right, wide ranging, entirely without form, without mind, no sense of self. If there is no self, there is no other. Therefore it is said, for the great commanders, there is no enemy. It is also said a man of virtue has no enemies." In this Toshiaki does not deviate at all from the classics. We may take this man of virtue to be a warrior, or indeed, a man in government service. The discussion of this art is not all clever words. It is a good explanation of this principle. Although this is a preface to a work on the Itto-ryu, the principles are, in fact, the same as those of the Shingyotou-ryu. In other words, you should realize from this that what I say always conforms to the principles of many schools. In the afterword to the *Kenjutsu Sho* the same writer also said, "And so when you teach, you learn and you develop your mind; when you develop your mind you become accomplished." This learning is study, this development becomes spontaneous. This is what is referred to in the saying, "Refine justice, continually keep it bright and you will receive inspiration." This kind of saying, too, may be from a different school, but it is the same. The more you know, the more you realize that many schools are the same.

There is a saying which goes, "You should season your voice backstage." This is very true. In general, nowadays, if someone is giving a lecture, when you look at the people who are sitting there listening, they will look very serious, but if you see them after they leave, they will take deep breaths, yawn, laugh, or whatever. In an instant they have switched their attention away from the lecture. They regard the lecture as public and normal life as private. This is how it resembles the saying.

As a seat at a lecture is where you learn something, it is like being backstage. Normal life is where you apply it—that is like the play. Because backstage is where you tune up, you are able to make adjustments. When you are on stage, this is not possible. You should consider this thoroughly. Thus, in the art of the sword, the practice hall is private, your normal life is public. If you think that excelling in practice is enough you have missed the point. You should distinguish between your practice as rehearsal, and your normal life as performance. As I said before, you can't redo your mistakes on the stage. The practice hall is where you have the opportunity to learn. Excellent swordsmen scrupulously separate practice from performance.

In swordsmanship there are also techniques you acquire in unusual situations. Generally when people are called they just answer "yes" and stand up, as everyone knows. Of course, this can be inappropriate manners in some cases. If your father called, you wouldn't respond like this. Nor if it was your teacher calling you. If we look at "just standing" in the dictionary "just" means "spontaneous." Although just an expression, in the language of my region we say "Ha" and stand up. To think of it another way, in this case the classification of father and teacher is unnecessary. "Respond" in the dictionary is an expression of replying. In the *Book of Rights** it says "If your father commands you, just obey, don't respond." In the commentary it notes that "just" is a formal way to say "quickly." "Respond" is slack and lazy.

Later, in the section on *touko*,† the master uses "respond." In the notes we can see this is associated with "listen attentively." Accordingly for "respond," now we would say "I understand," "I see what you mean," or "Certainly." Or in other words, it is an expression of acknowledgement that you have heard what someone said. If you take this distinction, just saying "yes" and standing up would be an empty mind in the

---

* *The Book of Rights (Liji)* by Confucius, one of the five Confucian classics.

† *Touko* was a popular game that involved throwing arrows into a pot.

art of the sword. To respond shows a "full" mind. If, for some reason, you don't need to take care to distinguish whether it is your father or teacher, and get up immediately, speaking without any particular care, this is equivalent to a defeat. With your father and teacher, there is an element of defeat from the first. We take a kamae carefully, although because we all have the attitude that we must serve our superiors, this does not appear to be so. From the first, to respond is not a bad thing. This was the line of argument about *kyu-jitsu*—full and empty—in the art of swordsmanship.

It's a provincial expression but, in the mundane world of a tea house, or a restaurant, for instance, serving women or man-servants will quickly reply when a customer calls them with, "yes, yes" or something similar—their mind is empty. The root of this "empty mind" is that there is no particular desire to answer. It is certainly because first and foremost it is important to respond to someone else that it is like this. From the first, when you catch the change described above and stand up with a "yes, yes," no one continues saying "yes, yes." After all, this would not be what the customer intended. If you have the original intention to "just respond" as in swordsmanship, doing everything fast, you will be able to distinguish both ends. If you can distinguish a response from just answering quickly, the changing condition of a full and empty mind, this is known as *nito*—double swords. If you can grasp the center, it will become the heart of these two things. If you think about this, is it not the road to certain victory?

The master always said, you should go beyond the importance of winning contests in the practice hall. On the contrary, your normal state is of primary importance. For that reason, during training you should make those techniques real. This is the essence of real contests. However, if you spend your time training moving the body pointlessly, without engaging the mind, it will amount to nothing. Recently, I was reading the *Rules of Propriety* in the *Book of Rites*, in which it says, "if you attend a mourning ceremony you will, of course, wear a suitable expression of sympathy, although usually you would smile because attending a ceremony is not normally a cause for grief." When you are dressed in full armor, your demeanor will be extremely forbidding. It is written, "Therefore a superior man is careful that his countenance does not unknowingly show any nuance of his true feelings." However men of the past had already gained this insight. Following their lead, for those who value courtesy, we might put the analogy forcefully and say this is the essence of swordsmanship. The characteristic of these examples is that they do not demonstrate naturalness. The wise certainly took care not to lower their guard. Swordsmen also think like this. When you face an opponent in the practice hall, taking care to strengthen your mental outlook, strive not to lose your look of indomitability.

Within the outer gatehouse of the castle there are placed what are called the three tools of the road*: one is the *hineri* (twister); the next is the *shumoku* (push pole); the last is the *sasumata* (forked pole). These three are widely known, and are required for use by foot soldiers. Among the lords of Ehime was a certain Kato who had some skill in the three tools. His style was the Ishida-ryu. I realized that even though these tools are kept inside the outer gates of the city to be used for control in times of emergency, soldiers never knew how to use them. I started to use his retainers in the Ishida-ryu who acted as teachers—I had my foot soldiers study this. Usually they developed some skill and periodically reviewed what they had learned. The defender often held the sword. From the beginning I had thought, it's not a fixed rule who has to hold

---

* These three tools are more commonly known as *sodegarami*, *tsukubo*, and *sasumata*.

the sword, but first in the case of a warrior holding the sword, as the three tools are for use by foot soldiers, swords should not be able to beat this technique at all. So doesn't this mean if a warrior comes up against a foot soldier who has trained in this technique, he shouldn't be able to beat him? Should leaders yield technique to foot soldiers? Should I submit? If you submit, the warrior's swordsmanship is unusable from the start. The public look on these tools as useless, but those who are ignorant shouldn't discuss them. Those who feel apprehensive when they look carefully at these techniques are very likely those who need to use caution with their sword techniques. There is no need for deliberation beyond this. In my school among the inner secrets there are mental techniques. If you know these, you will likely be able to handle this. Of old it was said "Possession of virtue is a treasure," but though this opinion appears to be different, in principle it is the same. However, those with only superficial understanding will find it difficult to see the similarity.

In the case of contests with other styles, people often say things like, "If I come up against someone who does that I'll use this technique," or people praise someone for winning. No doubt the one who is praised will think his technique is excellent, and that he will beat the same opponent in the future. I do not agree. According to the spirit of this school, a one-time victory is not a lifetime victory, which is to say that though you beat that person, you should not regard it as proof of superiority. Even though this is a secret, I'll put it here: in terms of victory, if your victory is a one-time victory, your technique is insignificant; if it is a permanent victory, your technique is settled. A swordsman who has a thorough understanding of this principle is able to learn the secrets of this school.

In *Mengzi* it says, "People turn to benevolence as water flows downwards and animals run to their burrows. So it is to the benefit of the deeps that the otter drives fish into them; for the benefit of the thicket that the falcon chases sparrows into it; for the benefit of Tang and Wu that Jie and Zhou* drove their people mercilessly." If we take an example from swordsmanship, if I am struck by someone, or beaten, it means my *kamae* is deficient. By reaching out with our hands we are hit or are beaten. However, the otter which aims at catching the fish from the start drives it into the deeps where it cannot be reached. We seek victory ourselves, taking various *kamae*, in the end suffering defeat; the otter chasing the fish, the falcon chasing the sparrow, Jie and Zhou driving their people mercilessly to side with Tang and Wu; this is the body that cannot move freely. Analyze this carefully. If you cannot understand, you will need oral instruction.

The Reverend Tojun (of Sho-o-ji temple), once spoke of Tokuhon,† who had achieved great virtue. Originally the child of a farmer in Kishu, (now Wakayama), he left home at 16. He had never studied formally, but from when he was a farmer he would diligently recite the *nembutsu*, going without sleep, building up his achievement in penance, which he would undertake in answer to whatever inquiry arose in his heart. One day a certain person told me, if Tokuhon is criticized, no matter who it is, no matter what they said, he places his hands together and prays for them, sincerely and gratefully. If someone asked what he was doing praying for him, he would say that this is for doing him wrong in the past. But listen carefully, sins will lead to ruin. Thus, when you ought to be aroused to anger, but you return it with goodness, this is a fine thing. Equally beneficial is the further insight I have gained into swordsmanship. When we are struck by an opponent, we

---

* Jie and Zhou: two legendary Chinese tyrants whose harsh policies led to successful revolts against them. Jie was the last king of Xia, (killed by Tang), and Zhou was King of Shang (killed by Wu).

† Tokuhon (1758–1818): an ascetic Buddhist priest known for his reciting of the *nembutsu*.

are normally sure to be angry. In my case it is not so. If I am struck by the opponent's technique it is owing to my clumsy form or, or if I have indulged, certainly that is where I have failed to follow the way. Therefore, one must, of course, ensure the form is correct, and with a sincere will pray that it does not differ from the *honshin*—original mind. You should test yourself for the space of a few years—herein lies the principle of victory. If you apply them, you may depend on the words and ideas of the ascetic Tokuhon. In addition, in the training hall, there is occasion to test these words: suppose you are injured through someone else's fault. Then, the injured person should turn to the person who struck him and bow to him. Essentially these contests of swordsmanship should not become emotional, but because of human nature, if someone is injured, it is natural to feel sympathy for them. But at the same time, the person who has struck the other should try to hide this as much as possible. The one who was hit should also try to master his bitterness as much as possible. Distinguished practitioners always conduct themselves well: if the unexpected occurs when they are attacking, if they are struck by their opponent for example, then they are happy, having made up their minds that this defeat is the way to future victory. And so, what Tokuhon said is what a teacher of this discipline should say too. You should resolve that the victory of today is not the victory of tomorrow; the benefit of one time is not the benefit of another. This is just one part of the instruction I received.

In the *Record of Linji** there appears the story of the Zen teacher Fuke.† In it there is the following verse:

---

* The *Linji-lu* is a collection of the lectures and sermons of Linji (d.866), founder of one of the major schools of Chan (Zen) Buddhism. Linji is more well-known in the Japanese reading of his name, Rinzai.

† Fuke (Puhua): a somewhat eccentric contemporary of Linji and founder of the Fuke Zen school.

When it comes in brightness, I strike the brightness.
When it comes in darkness, I strike the darkness.
When it comes from the four quarters and the eight direc-
tions I strike like a whirlwind.
If it comes from the empty sky, I strike like a flail.

Even though this story illustrates the meaning of Zen, men
who are skilled in the sword fully understand what it means.
Strike like a whirlwind, or in other words, I bring disorder to
all around me. Strike like a flail, if you compare the fury of the
outer limb with the center you should be able to understand
properly. It is probably difficult to understand the original intention at first.

In my humble opinion, in swordsmanship, thrusting the
sword forward is, if you consider its speed and force, really a
killing sword. Again, if you draw your sword back, although
you are aware it's ineffectual against people, it really is a sword
of life. Whatever you call it, a person who thrusts, despite this
speed and force, finds that at its furthest extent it is difficult to
change. Therefore it is a dead sword. When you draw it back
the force is weak, but if you blend, when it has reached the
point of greatest extent, you will certainly be able to change.
What is change? If you stab, sweep, turn, or cut it can become
any one of these. And this is why it is a living sword. If you
have any doubts about this, you will need to have it explained
to you in person.

However, later, on looking through the chapter on *Month-
ly Rituals** I saw that it says, "Now it is this month (May) the
days are becoming longer. It is the struggle of Yin and Yang. It
is part of life and death. A superior man purifies himself and
at the right time secludes himself in silence." This spirit, of the
moon of May, is that as the days get longer, and yet longer, the

---

* In the *Liji* (*Book of Rites*).

Yang energy will be full. You should bear it in mind that because it is full, from then it will decrease, steadily becoming weaker. Then yin will be visible, and even though it's not yet strong it will begin to increase greatly. That's why it is called a struggle between yin and yang—this is the same as the concept that a big person is not necessarily strong, a small person not weak. Thus swordsmanship contains the same principle. In the *Liji*, it says, "Adhere to heaven and earth in all matters, whatever they are; if you do not depart from the ways of heaven and earth, you can find the principle even in a minor way like the sword." Even though it is difficult and sounds strange, if you think about it hard, there is nothing strange about it. With yin and yang, though fullness is fast and strong, from this comes the path of decrease. Slight of speed and weak though it may be, from here is the path to their extreme. Thus it is known as the place between life and death. It is also known as the body of the May moon. A superior person knows this and is aware that things such as purification embody the principle of heaven and earth, which is the control of the body. In swordsmanship too, when young you possess vigor and depend on force; for someone who is more developed, this approach is the same as knowing nothing about *ki* and having no control; though you seek victory the reverse will occur and you will taste defeat. Victory is life; defeat is only death.

Again, in the commentaries on the *Liji* it says, "Purifying yourself you regulate your mind; secluding yourself you protect your body. This is 'not behaving carelessly.'" This matches the teaching of swordsmanship. If you don't understand you need oral instruction.

Among my lowly peers, there are some who are very knowledgeable in art. One day, one of them asked about the paintings of Chinese people, in which some of them wear swords on their backs. I answered, I don't know about the method of the

Tang,* but as you say, they do wear them like that. In that style, the hilt of the sword sticks up above the wearer's right shoulder, the tip is at the lower back on the left, with the cord tied so that one end comes from the right shoulder, the other from the left hip, wrapping across the body. At one time, a retainer following his mounted lord would always station himself at the horse's left shoulder. If he favored that style, when he stepped forward with his right foot, his left foot would open out, he would lean forward, putting power into his hips as he advanced his right shoulder. This made it easy for his lord to draw the sword from a mounted position. If he wanted to draw himself, while on foot, then what he would do would be to assume the same position as before, holding his *saya*† in the left hand, push it up, grasp the hilt as it rose above his shoulder, then pull the *saya* with his left hand, which allowed him to draw and cut with his right hand. On occasions this style would be adopted—it is no different from drawing the sword that is worn at the waist. I actually tried it myself and it was no different from what I expected. The questioners were delighted. From among them one said he heard about this when in a Korean military camp. According to the opinions of that country, the swords that our fellow countrymen wear at their waist leave them open when they first draw. When someone with their sword on their back, their right hand by their head, draws and strikes towards the neck, being aware that our countrymen will strike upwards from the hip, this allows the enemy to sever their elbows as they cut upwards. They said they can win time and time again.

I say, by all means, let them come.

---

* Meaning China.
† *Saya*: the sheath of a sword

Ignorance In Swordsmanship
(*Kenjutsu Fushiki Hen*)

Kimura Kyuhou

Preface

There is a natural path in the world, but people do not know it. If they knew it, they would, perhaps, be called sages. Perhaps spontaneity is what is also called energy in harmony with heaven. The swordsmanship that was passed down to me is called the Unchu-ryu; its ancestor was Itou Nyudo Kii Suketada of Oushuu Province who mastered the subtleties of the art of the spear, first disciplining himself in the *kuda yari*.[*] Subsequently the *naginata* was added by Ogasahara Naiki Sadaharu, the straight spear and cross-bladed spear by Torao Monemon Mitsuyasu, and these have been handed down through the generations. But the teachers of recent times, though they now bear illustrious titles, have yet to achieve the highest levels. My teacher embarked on this path and spent year after year in solitary training, concealing his heart and deepening his thinking. After many years he naturally achieved this level, after which he had developed such free-

---

[*] A type of spear that utilizes a short metal tube (*kuda*) through which the shaft slides.

dom that he was able to move as if his opponent was not there at all. Truly, it should be said that this famous teacher revived this school. Going to other provinces, he stimulated interest among many warriors: among a thousand students there were four or five who were capable of attaining these principles. I invited them to study with me, he said. Long ago, this style had the straight spear and cross-bladed spear added to it. Now it also includes the long sword. Our teachers' blessings have been passed down over the years, he told his students. It is my hope that this may be continued. Accordingly Rinjitsu entrusted it to his students. Thus he is the founder of the long sword style of this school.

I came into contact with my teacher about the time I entered manhood. I could not absorb all he had to teach. The technique was a mere drop in the ocean. One day, a visitor arrived and discussed the strengths and weaknesses of the various schools. I was waiting in attendance beside them and listened, deeply impressed: I have set down the words here just as I heard them. However, I deeply regret that in my sixty years I have been unable to master the whole art. For this reason I have called this single volume that I have produced, "Ignorance in Swordsmanship." And so, to show my childish ignorance, I want to leave this to my descendants. It is my sole intention to continue the art that I received from my teacher. For those that hope to follow this art for their future happiness, if you examine this it should be of some little help. Though it brings death, it enhances life still more. This is something I aspire to myself. My teacher's family name was Hori; his personal name Rinjitsu and his title Kindayuu. He was a native of Nobeoka in Nisshyuu in Shikoku. His ancestors were lords of Arima, so from his youth, he was in service and went to Echizen, together with his lord. After some 66 or 67 years he died in the 5th year of Houreki (1755) on the 12th day of the 10th month. His disciples grieved as though they had lost a parent. After his death he was given the posthumous name Toumon as a lay Buddhist of Ryushin-in temple.

> Humbly written by the student Kimura Kyuhou
> on the 12th day of the 10th month,
> in the 1st year of Meiwa (1764).

~

The visitor said, "Master, you have distilled a single principle of swordsmanship from emptiness. Although what you say is quite right, it is said to be very advanced and difficult to achieve for the inexperienced. Though unusually talented individuals may make progress, in just perfecting a single principle, saying you need only discard what you have learned sounds like a monk on the road to enlightenment tampering with a sword; the clumsy motions of the mind won't help attain this state. Since long ago, the great commanders watched the unsophisticated techniques of provincials, or military training, to no small effect. On the contrary, these esteemed figures said you should not rid yourself of this unsophistication. Similarly you should not ignore the shallows you cross to reach the depths, or tramp heedlessly over the foothills to reach the heights—just follow the principle. What you should do at first is simply apply yourself to what you have been taught and the principle will develop naturally."

The master replied, "what you say is very reasonable. In terms of guiding the inexperienced, I do just as you say. However that may be, I don't teach choreographed patterns. Therefore, among those who are unfamiliar with it, there are many who regard this as just a theoretical art. It is difficult for someone who has not entered the school to understand. With choreographed patterns, everyone performs moves that are pre-arranged—this is not realistic. Therefore, at the beginning, while they do learn patterns for a while, I do not teach them for long. After that I instruct them realistically. If there is any divergence from principle in this technique, it is solely as a foundation for proceeding in the art based on the path of this single principle. It is not necessary to discard anything. Therefore we engage in practice with the bamboo sword, the spear, and the *naginata*. If you discard things, surely you could not practice with the spear, with the sword, and so on. You should be able to understand this. What are called techniques in the wider world are only pre-arranged set patterns. This school does not make use of such pre-arranged patterns, or learn set forms. The practical techniques that have been extracted from the principle are shown by utilizing the path of spontaneous response.

"First, when you start, there is an opening, which allows you to take the first steps to understanding the one principle. Gradually you are swept up in and comply with this principle, your mind becomes calm and you are filled with energy. In a natural progression, your fears drop away, then as you press forward into danger and you are forced to adopt all sorts of positions, cuts, and thrusts against your opponent, then I teach students techniques which incorporate the principle of emptiness, pressing forward, and then the principle of emptiness and the 'moon in the water' combine and they will come to understand how to read the opponent's intention through emptiness. When they acquire this skill, they will be able to draw themselves into and blend with the opponent's pressure. This is the heart of the Yagyu School. When they have perfected the initial points above and beyond this, delved deeply into the *shinjutsu* (techniques of the mind and spirit) they will have detachment from life and death, and techniques and theory will both have been discarded. When you have discarded techniques and theory, it is called *mushin* or 'no-mind.' When you achieve 'no-mind' the mind and body just respond spontaneously as things happen. You can enter this state at will. Having already achieved technical and theoretical mastery, you will naturally come to be able to see the opponent's level clearly, his strengths and weaknesses and the path to victory. There is no situation nor class of men in all creation to which this way cannot be applied. Surely this is what the masters of ancient times possessed. Though this has not been made known to the public at large, if all things arise from it, cannot, therefore, the one principle be made clear? First learn the art of the spear, then discard everything—is this not the correct sequence?"

The visitor said, "there are undoubtedly other ways to achieve this advanced level. I'm not ready to accept what you said. All the various houses differentiate beginners from intermediate students by the number of patterns they know, and when they progress to an advanced level there are still many more advanced patterns for the sword. To start with, the teacher must not be humble. At first, if we discuss worldly matters, as one goes from a lowly samurai to a man of responsibility, often calling on magistrates, and then becoming a leader, paying close attention to issues of administration will certainly be of great benefit. However, after you thoroughly understand worldly duties, why should you not teach from established examples?"

The master answered, "your innocent belief in progressing from basic to difficult, which in swordsmanship means the use of choreographed set patterns, is quite reasonable, as it is the method adopted by the majority of teachers. Be that as it may, Kino Nyudo, the founder of this school, like Master Yagyu Munenori* of Washu and Miura Masanari† of Busho,

---

* Yagyu Munenori (1571–1646): a famous master of the Yagyu Shinkage-ryu.

† Miura Masanari (fl.1680s): founder of the Mugan-ryu. His name is often written as Miura Masatame.

the founder of the Mugan style, honored his domain; and he too transcended various schools, old and new. Taking two or three disciples he went to spy on the various schools in Tobu. All of them employed paired kata and there were none who had achieved outstanding skill. Among those who showed little understanding were those orthodox teachers who created and taught choreographed patterns. Although it is said this makes it easy to understand and refine the principles of the style, the results should bear this out. They are unable to lead anyone to realization of the principle. After a certificate of accomplishment is awarded in a tradition where attainment is measured by progress in choreographed patterns, it is not likely that you will come to your senses. There is neither sign nor shape of the truth. Therefore there is no doubt of the difficulty in initiating someone who has achieved this level. And so, from the start, the beginners mind should be gradually developed allowing them to gain some sense of the principle: by means of the empty (*kyo*) they will develop the real (*jitsu*). At first they will sense the principle only dimly, like a thread or a mist, but accumulating insights, they will discover progress, achieving both technical and theoretical understanding. This is skill.

"Eventually you have thoroughly mastered the principle, reaching a state beyond the physical. This may be called the Great Ultimate, or the Limitless Great Path. It is this that the masters should be passing on. When you reach this level, you will be still and unmoving without straying into defensiveness; not relying on your eyes and ears, but feeling and responding directly, because this virtue embodies a divine ferocity. However, even if they are guided along the orthodox path, the experienced still have the natural human desire for victory and to avoid defeat. In a situation where they are taught only to win, the arrogance of human desire becomes ever more firmly entrenched, their appearance is strained, if I am confused, my understanding is clouded; if I am angry, my compassion is lost; if I am frightened, my courage is broken; if I deceive, the truth is lost. This disturbance is as though a neighboring house has caught fire: you will certainly not come anywhere near a state of calm imperturbability. You will have spent a whole lifetime engaged in conflict. In principle, people with essentially the same nature should feel an affinity, so it is a sorry business if you think only of beating those you should love. If the true mind is clouded like this, instead of fostering malice, give up the drive to be first. You should simply adopt an underlying attitude of loyalty and filial respect. However accomplished you become in swordsmanship even if you learn enough to beat all the people in the world and though you may look violent, when you have a spirit of loyalty and filial respect, on finding yourself in a dangerous situation, you will, at once, forget old grudges and happily join forces, without the slightest attempt to slip out of it.

"But if you lack this kind of fidelity to principle, what use is it to habitually train yourself in the sword? Therefore Confucius said, 'Should not a warrior treasure humility in all his actions?' As a samurai departs from humility so should he forfeit the loyalty of his retainers. In such times of disturbance, the principle of fidelity appears and there will be no diminishing of military renown. The person who uses both normality and danger for the benefit of his country will surely be a valued warrior. All those who would do otherwise should be despised as brutes.

"To move on to your example of worldly affairs, even in the most extreme cases there are two alternative approaches. As you said, at first a person of some youth who has worked for ten years or so will first be a foot soldier, then a junior officer, a warrior, a leader of a troop, a general, a magistrate, a court official, and so on. Walking this single path to its end, he may later become a liege lord developing discernment in matters high and low—you are probably of the opinion that this calm is particularly helpful in achieving victory. Those with superficial knowledge and shallow opinions all share this belief. This goes beyond the principle, but is of no practical use. On this path and others of similar nature, men progress from youth, receiving gradually weightier appointments, leading to positions as leaders and magistrates, till they grow old in the service of the province, though finding precious little profit in the service of the way, they are finally broken for the sake of the state. On top of which, when you look into each and every phenomenon one at a time, is there anyone capable of thoroughly grasping them all, even if they had one or two lifetimes at their disposal? But if a person willingly takes the path of understanding the universal principle, they should be able to understand by themselves without exhaustive investigation into each and every thing.

"When Zhuge Liang* left his hermitage he took the welfare of the nation into his hands; the founder of China,† aroused from his sleep pacified the kingdom and founded a dynasty that lasted for 200 years. There are many examples of this kind from Japan. If you find this great path, the extent of this superfluity naturally becomes clear. However, if you long to reach the state where you can understand all things through the thorough understanding of just one, taking the long way round is like 'taking the narrow by-ways and stopping to smell the flowers.' Someone else who had no liking for the practice of fixed choreographed patterns, Yagyu Munenori, likened them to the government. 'As I lead the inexperienced, the foot hills are passed over and the heights are reached, which is to say, you attempt to stride forward along a straight path, without stopping midway—reaching the capital becomes your princi-

---

* Zhuge Liang (181–234): famous strategist from the period of the Three Kingdoms.

† The legendary Huang-di, or Yellow Emperor.

pal aim. It is as though you were the Shogun and possessed a jewel that gave you knowledge of the whole kingdom.'

"In the *Chapter on Government* in the *Analects of Confucius* it says, 'Suppose the North Star were to appear here: the other stars would all turn to face towards it.' If we apply this to the sword, around the central position are arrayed 80,000 swords. The center is the same 'level' as immovable. The Confucian teachings are also settled around the center. In the Great Learning it says, 'Virtue is made clear. This Great Ultimate appears at the beginning, pointing out to the novice scholar, who proceeds in his study from the bottom with this as the object, understanding of the status of things is achieved. Sincere in intention, of just mind, if the student is taught, he will be illuminated by the virtue of the target.'

"In swordsmanship, too, if the virtue of the universal principal is taught as a goal from the start, using this as a basis for practice, the universal principal of emptiness can be sought. Therefore, even in a dirty backstreet, the principle appears from material things; first comes the technique—the principle appears later. However, if you look at what you have achieved, the reverse is true, the technique arises from the theory. How can this be? For theory, if we substitute the principle that existed before the creation of Heaven and earth, the technique is equivalent to the 3 powers* that arose subsequently. However, the principle is the root; the technique is the end. If you reach the heights from the lowlands, the landscape you see on your journey, the produce, the geography, the character of the people and so forth, will be visible in their entirety. The mind that lags behind, finally coming to a halt, will certainly develop partialities on the journey. Not only that, the scenery you encounter will color the inner principles and knowledge, and later, as a teacher, these errors will be passed on to all

* Heaven, earth, and man.

your successive students, which must be the saddest thing of all."

The visitor said, "other schools talk a great deal about concepts such as selflessness, no-mind, simple mind and each school stresses its particular principle. Why surely this is no different from the level of beasts?"

The master replied, "if there were not two principles there should be no difference with the other schools. But, when it comes to what are called principles, though the mind understands, when they are spoken, they all sound equal—but when you have a weapon in your hands and test the principle, you cannot tell if it is true or false. Furthermore, each of the various schools has their own theory, not a few of which sound profound. So when they are differentiated like this, people are confused. The bounds placed upon these schools' principles limit them. In this respect, if you value the correct principle, none of the other schools will lead you there: their principles are one-sided and not completely rounded out. Thus they are minor arts. 'A refined man,' it is said, 'first sees all and remains impartial; the small man is biased and cannot see all.' Again to make a comparison, it's as if a group of blind men are assembled, taken to an elephant and asked to describe its form just from what they have felt. The one who felt its back says it's like a mat on the floor; the one who felt its tail says it's like a rope; the one who felt its tusk says it's like a horn, and the one who felt its leg says it's like a pillar. Because they're blind and their answers can't encompass the whole body—they just say what they felt. The principles of all the different schools when they talk about their advantages are, in fact, like this. Because the true principle is something we cannot see with our eyes, the various schools contain bias and so disagree with each other.

If you are aware of the huge difference in appearances occasioned by the flexibility of the principle, there will be neither disagreement nor confusion—thus all will be equal. As to being on the level of beasts, small people are only like small creatures of the fields, who all believe they will triumph over people of the same character. In fact, already debased and corrupted by the Tengu* world of vanity and lies, will they not become veritable beasts? If they don't leave behind these outer delusions they grasp so tenaciously, their bodies will become brutish. They will become so-called 'beasts in human form.' So how on earth can this kind of brute corrupt the mind of an upright person?"

The visitor said, "master, you said that experts will not argue because of their knowledge of the way. But the top student of Yagyu Munenori, the master of old, in works such as the *Honshiki Sanmondou*,† poured scorn on other schools. And more recently, Mugan Miura's descendant Otsuka Yoshioki, wrote the *Kenjutsu Ron*, in which he heaps ridicule on other styles. Now, what you have said is again the same. Is this not disagreement. Indeed, this is looking down on what others do while doing the same thing yourself. In fact is this not conceited and hypocritical?"

The master replied, "if you are yourself armed, how can you criticize others for doing the same? Therefore, in just a minute, I will disentangle the rights and wrongs of your question. The Yagyu or the Mugan schools surely have no wish to impugn any other worthy styles. But those who train in choreographed set patterns do not develop skill; mistaking the path, they gradually stray in the darkness. It's like looking for fish in a tree. After spending your whole life in persisting

---

* Tengu were supernatural beings said to live in the mountains. They were traditionally connected with asceticism and some of the schools of martial arts, but here the reference is to their role as agents of disorder and delusion as enemies of Buddhism.

† *Honshiki Sanmondou (Three Questions and Answers on Essential Knowledge)*. Kimura published this work together with his own *Unchu-ryu Kenjutsu Youryou (Essentials of Unchu-ryu swordsmanship)* in 1752. The writer was probably Kimura Sukekurou Tomoshige (1580-1656).

in a mistake, you will sigh at what little you have seen of true virtue. This shows those people who are attached to the world. And again, it is in the axioms of my school,

> You will differentiate between yourself and others for a short time only. Since you do not have skill in a reasonable and acceptable art mistakes will naturally be apparent in your performance.

"It's just that when someone has explained the truth, you should not debate whether it's right or wrong. Although it may be said that a lack of understanding resembles dispute, swordsmanship is a path in which discussion can never decide victory. In other schools there are, no doubt, masters too. In many schools, the masters of previous generations must have been highly skilled, however the succeeding generations produced unworthy teachers who, having mistaken the principle, could not contest without choreographed patterns and fixed movements. And further, among those who followed were many who were incompetent. Of the eighteen styles of Miura, none of his teachers showed conformity of theory and principle. In those days, a considerable number of teachers of other schools allowed me to visit, but I have yet to see one person who possesses real skill. I gained some understanding of people from these investigations, and concluded that masters in this world are rare. If theory and technique conform in neither scholarship nor art, what kind of benefits do they confer? What I say is not something I believed from the start; I just came to develop this negative point of view."

The visitor said, "since long ago, many schools favored contests and a considerable number of swordsmen traveled the country in the course of their training. And men such as these were not inferior to Yagyu and Miura, yet somehow they remained obscure."

The master answered, "those traveling around the country to advance their training should be seen as two kinds. One is the person who is devoted to martial arts, year after year learns the highest techniques yet even so has not realized the one principle of complete victory. There are famous teachers in neighboring provinces he wants to meet in order to learn those subtle techniques. People of this sort may fight contests with various schools in different provinces: they are not pleased when they win, but when they suffer defeat; they feel that by beating those inferior to them they gain nothing. They are happy to lose; it means they have found someone who can beat them. In other words, they embarked on their training to meet people who were superior to them in order to learn their advanced techniques. Eventually, on achieving this principle, they would feel great humility in having reached this level of achievement, and so do not seek to be widely known. Those with this true devotion will show this kind of gratitude.

"The other kind based on contests of two or three schools, proclaim their own speed, intelligence and ability while ridiculing those accomplished in the arts, desiring to beat those of other provinces and schools and establish a reputation. These people are the opposite of those I mentioned previously. They are pleased when they win, downcast when they lose—people like this deviate from virtue and never obtain the way. After all, anyone who bears grudges and seeks to harm others will, ourselves included, suffer a violent death. These people fit the way to match their art. They are not devoted to the truth. The beasts we mentioned before regard their art as a means of establishing a reputation. Surely an unskilled novice is superior to this. When you have reached the highest level of swordsmanship, even though you don't fight you achieve victory spontaneously. While winning through strategy without fighting is advanced, and fighting to achieve victory is the core, should not winning while teaching be considered the lowest level? Because the principal is something that is insubstantial, even though it is before your very eyes, it is hard to see. That is why you see those who are devoted travel around the provinces. Once they discover the one principle, what good is traveling around the provinces? It is not necessary to wait for recognition from others, that is enough for them. It is like the saying, 'Poets know about famous places without leaving their dwellings.'"

The visitor then said, "master, what you have said is completely in the realm of mental and spiritual technique—it is not swordsmanship at all. Just training the spirit without trying to win is not the same thing as achieving enlightenment from studying the sutras and sacred writings. Through swordsmanship you can only gain an incomplete understanding."

The master replied, "although what we call 'single mindedness' may be inferior to full understanding, it's a state you can't achieve unless you practice the sword. Originally swords were not to be used as dangerous weapons. However, when used properly, they would help bring good fortune to society. So, in other words, by wielding a killing sword you have a sword of life. It is also true that swordsmanship is a minor art. How can it be a spiritual path? However you put it, I was born into a warrior family, so if I am to do my duty, practicing the arts of sword and spear, on reaching an understanding of the principle, the family arts will not be in vain. Furthermore, though lacking in academic talent, we put it into practice and were able to achieve the true way. In this way it becomes a major way. And so we ask what it is. Because there is an opponent with a sword in swordsmanship, when there are too many distracting signs, we blame the opponent. This sword wielding opponent is, in fact, a living book. At times like this, though swordsmanship seems like a spiritual path, it is actually very far from it. It is just that you are expanding it because you have reached a level where you can comprehend a spiritual path.

In general, if you practice them as ways, neither swordsmanship, academic studies, Shinto writings, nor Buddhist sutras will grant you spiritual realization. Through practicing these disciplines you will attain spiritual understanding only if you have reached the way.

"Although I am only dealing with swordsmanship, if you ignore the name it applies to all arts. Sunzi said, 'To win one hundred victories in one hundred battles is not the highest of achievements. When you can win without fighting, you will have acquired the principle of invincibility.' Of course, if it does not contain an inner component, how can the virtue of all things be made clear? However skilled you become with the sword, if it is not under control when you meet the enemy your whole mind will be in confusion. Even the most basic things will slip from your grasp. With swordsmanship, what is most fundamental is that you should have knowledge of the sword at your waist. Why on earth would you not want to apply yourself to it? When your original mind is understood, you can treat life and death with equanimity. When meeting an opponent you will be as normal, your mental state will not collapse and, imitating nothing, you will be able to move freely. In general, in swordsmanship, thinking about defeating other people is the attitude of an inferior person. Indeed, it also equates to being defeated yourself. In this state, though you have a multitude of victories, they are all lucky wins. It is not what we call invincibility. Just discipline yourself in the principle with an unobstructed mind; the solitary person will certainly obtain invincibility.

"According to the reckoning of Heaven, we will die, but as if at ease, this death will have a proper beauty. The brave warrior will not forget to mourn the past; he who has become a warrior will achieve goodness through bravely facing life and death. Therefore great commanders, on facing death, do nothing unseemly. Composed, they face death with the same grace they bring to elegant pursuits. Thus they exhibit *mushin* with regard to death, as well as to life. The brave, virtuous warrior, though he wishes to live, will not stain his virtue. By abandoning his body, he becomes virtuous. This is exactly the same as the sage who, treating life and death as equal, commits to the path of death when there is death, and when there is life, commits to the path of life. When this occurs, you can live freely and die at will."

The visitor said, "many schools practice adjusting the cutting distance and sometimes in the pre-arranged patterns there are two or three cuts. Also, without an attacker, measuring the distance ourselves we swing the sword one hundred or one thousand times in cutting practice every day. I have heard that without establishing the distance and cutting, swordsmanship is ineffective. Do you not do this in your style?"

In answer, the master said, "in my style from beginners to the inner levels, as long as you strike with the long sword, there is no occasion in which distance is not established. 'Distance' is the distance between us and the opponent; it is the theory of space. In my style, showing the principle of space is what is commonly known as 'distance.' But, when you have no attacking partner and just swing the sword alone, one or two thousand times, day after day, it is difficult to appreciate. And what's more, this is not distance. In deciding, will you determine the grip, or should you exclusively concentrate on the efficacy of the strike? If that is so, this is what you will surely do first. If you depart from this fixed distance, you will learn nothing. Again, it is extremely inadvisable to set your distance, and defend against the enemy's attacks like this. The distance I teach has no limit when it stretches; when it shortens, it is closer than a hair's breadth. Both stretching and closing, if you are close to the enemy or far it is the mastery of being neither too much nor too little. In this way, if the principle is without guile, we develop excess and insufficiency. If you reach the level of 'meeting the arrow with the sword,' the term 'distance' is not used. Distance is the name given to the relationship of opposing objects. When you reach the level of no self, no enemy, you should understand that the intention of 'distance' is the same as confusion. What good will it do you to practice what other schools call 'distance' on your own, striking strongly enough to break through an iron wall, concentrating on the grip and effectiveness, if you are too close or too far? Surely it is hardly any use at all."

The visitor said, "many other schools have traditions that are passed down orally. Why is it not so in your school, master?"

The master replied, "this is exactly what swordsmanship with choreographed patterns has in abundance. This way of transmitting teachings is good for beginners. It is difficult to use for intermediate to more advanced students. Why is it that these teachers strive so? It is not that they are bad, but rather again and again they hit on ideas to be more effective. If that's the case, it's obvious they derive these teachings completely from human understanding. The virtue of this school's principle of appearing empty is connected to the spirit. It certainly cannot be achieved by means of the intellect. As for how to learn this, Sanskrit characters, *kuji* and *juji gohou*, *inmyou** and so on, were learnt from Buddhists and passed on to the disciples. But then, even if you believe this is unquestionably the correct theory, if there is someone, for example, who enjoys beating people, or uses this to harm people, or again, is greedy, this should not be done indiscriminately. Similarly, it can be exceedingly dangerous to entrust the higher levels of swordsmanship. In all events, this is the way such a school will decline in refinement. Therefore, when someone

---

* *Kuji* (9 character) and *juji* (10 character) *gohou*, and *inmyou* are all esoteric practices said to confer practical benefits on the practitioner, and utilized in some schools of martial arts.

has reached the more advanced levels without obtaining the level of the one principle of emptiness and the subtle spirit, they cannot teach this to their own students, and so they teach a number of choreographed patterns and forms over and over, and at the extreme level, pass on such things as curses in oral instruction. When they have finished learning and mastering these various things, there is nothing more. These schools will decline without fail.

"For example, if we take the government of a province, they seem bound to pass many laws. When the sage governs the world, we hear there are no more than three laws. It appears from the writings of the Yagyu school, that their teachings are as numerous as grains of sand on the beach, but after all though you can swallow all the water of the West River in a single gulp,* if you are forced to do everything the result will be very clumsy. So it is said, the ten thousand schools are all small streams. If only based on a single river, your view will be extremely limited when you debate the strengths and weaknesses of all the other schools. If you discipline yourself and desire the great waters of the West River quickly, you should swallow the water of all the many streams in a single gulp. If everything arose from a single thing, if you can grasp this original single thing, which is to be without desire, without ego, then you will have a clear understanding of all things.

"We have the sword of worship, of asceticism, and as spiritual armor. Beyond this, there are spells which cause fever, spirit possession by foxes, curses of stopping the blood, pulling out fish bones and all sorts of other curses besides; even if these have been of some help in the world and they might be good to know, how will they ever be of any help in swordsmanship? However doing these suspicious kinds of things and applying them to swordsmanship is a laughable notion.

---

* A reference to a Zen koan alluding to instantaneous enlightenment or intuitive understanding.

What is called wickedness is not the enemy of righteousness. Stick to the correct method: it is free of mystery. This form of wickedness cannot be used on those who hold to the truth: it is like ice melting in the sun. Those who have not clearly understood this principle are in a state of puzzlement and folly. Nevertheless, though disciples are in the midst of increasing folly, they faithfully receive instruction. This depends on faith in the unknown as well their desire for the benefits. In my school the passing on of handed down transmissions is not enough. Just doing is the transmission. Having embarked on the way, loyalty is the kind of attitude that will aid you."

The guest said, "master, when you teach, you have said you dislike choreographed fixed patterns, though a critic might say for techniques when you are pressed close for example, you respond to the enemy's position, his strikes and thrusts, and this too probably seems like an example of choreographed patterns. And so in such a *kamae* (guard), you should attack at an angle, and if you strike at an angle, you should respond like so, for that position there is this technique and its variations, there is undoubtedly all sorts of knowledge of this kind. So relying on choreographed patterns, guessing the enemy's mind, is this not the way you teach the inexperienced?"

In answer the master said, "even though what you said is similar on the whole, the way I teach is very unusual. Many schools alike have upper, middle, and lower positions as well as *kamae* such as *aisute, seigan, setsukabuto*˙ (helmet splitting), and so forth, to name but a few, and who knows how many variations there must be. And beyond this, I do not know the number of inner and outer refinements. Many other

---

˙ *Aisute, seigan, setsukabuto*: three different *kamae*: although *kamae* differ slightly from style to style, each school had *kamae* in which the sword was held in an upper, middle, and lower position. Here the terms denote a position facing the opponent side on, with the sword tip lowered, pointing to the rear; a standard position, with the sword held at roughly navel height, the tip pointing at the opponent; the sword raised, pointing upwards with the hands at head height.

schools have a liking for filling the mind with all sorts of these things, and for those aspects beyond the reach of conscious consideration they appear to use religious doctrines, *inmyou*, and so forth. This is a serious weakness in swordsmanship, the ultimate fallacy. When the mind is burdened like this, it is in a continual state of agitation. Afterwards, without the appearance of virtue, knowledge and insight conflict, and contrary to the intended purpose it becomes difficult to project the mind as it is. It is reflected at the moment glances are exchanged, but does nothing to decide victory and defeat; subsequently you will develop into someone of no great ability.

"In this world of violence and bloodshed, we have probably heard of such cases as revenge for lords or parents. This knowledge becomes the cloak of virtue. With this the mysterious spirit does not rise. In the *Six Classics** it says, 'Great Wisdom is not wise; great benevolence is not kind; great courage is not bold. Just following natural laws, natural wisdom, natural benevolence, natural bravery: if immense virtue, it cannot be seen by narrow-minded people. If you have this, it will be said, without wisdom, without benevolence, without courage.' *The Doctrine of the Mean*† states, 'The superior man is quiet and calm and waits for what life brings; the small-minded man walks in dangerous places seeking lucky chance.'

"When I guide, first I leave behind wisdom, when I show you what the principle of emptiness looks like, it proceeds from a natural level. As above, you wait for what comes, the opponent can take whatever *kamae* he may choose, using a method suited for that *kamae*, you strike from within the principle of emptiness. Again, even when the opponent changes, you don't use your faculties of careful discernment and consideration, just adapt to each change directly, not meeting the

---

* The six Confucian classics.

† *The Doctrine of the Mean* (*Zhongyong*) is part of *The Book of Rites* (*Liji*) and is attributed to Zisi, the grandson of Confucius.

whites of his eyes even a little. Giving up the idea of judgment and analysis, adapting to the changes seems 'divine,' because it is a state of *mushin, muchaku*—no-mind, no-attachment, just the principle of emptiness—which allows your natural characteristics to shine in all directions. When you come to cross swords with the enemy, the time for thinking is already past. Thus, without judgement, becoming free, my students can take part in practice from when they are beginners. As the profound virtue described above develops, mental judgment is used less and less. As the opponent adopts different positions, your own body does not move: *hassou* is *hassou, seigan* is *seigan, sha* is *sha;*[*] just seeing it as it is, without judgment. In harmony with the single principle, supported by virtue, when you are in *mushin*, the opponent finds himself unable to move or take the initiative. In this respect, those who act on the principle say it was clearly the work of something mysterious, 'I' did not do it. And so, compared to other schools, the way I teach is quite unusual. And that is why those who are competitive as beginners do not value this school. There are many who give up practice voluntarily. It's a far cry from the study of choreographed patterns, in which spontaneity will not be achieved because the mind and the form are both already decided. In this school the form, the sword and the mind are not pre-set and so there is spontaneity. Those who have only technique without seeing the principle are like a dog which goes round and round the post it is chained to."

The guest said, "the mind is the key to mastering the spirit of winning with one cut. You should not desire to depart from the mind. If you are in a state of no-mind, not using your mind, can this actually be swordsmanship?"

The master replied, "yes indeed. There is nothing other than the spirit of the single cut. That being the case, the mind

---

* These *kamae* correspond to the three mentioned above: *hassou* is an upper *kamae, sha* is an alternative term for *aisute*, a lower *kamae*.

that you speak of is ego. The non-mind that I refer to is the original mind. The original mind has no form, no color, no smell, and no shadow. This is *mushin*. In this original mind, the spirit in which inside and out are in perfect accord with the essential emptiness is also known as the single principle of the true ultimate. The ego has shadow and form, colored from its contact with the world. When you use the ego, you cannot exert yourself in all directions. When you use *mushin*, you return to the one principle, clear and pure, inside and outside, unstained by anything, untainted by the world.

"Laozi said, 'By virtue of this principle the heavens are thereby clear and pure; Earth is stable and the spirits divine. All in the world is constant because of it. Without it, the heavens would not be clear. If they were not clear, they would be split asunder. If the earth was not stable, it would warp and crack, if the spirits had no souls, they would be impotent; if the valleys were not fertile, they would become exhausted; if all creatures were not filled with the spirit of life, they would perish. If the kings and lords were not correct, they would stumble.' Swordsmanship that attains one-ness is a clear expression of the spirit. Therefore it responds to change freely, without hindrance. If this one-ness has not been obtained there is no strongly trained spirit. If there is no such spirit, the technique and the theory are both obscured. When they are obscured, he and I are not clearly differentiated. When they are not differentiated, they become two. When they are two, there is conflict. When there is conflict, there is victory and defeat. It is also said, 'The Tao produces one; one gives birth to two; two gives birth to three; and from three comes all creation. Everything returns to the one. The one is the Great Ultimate. Two is heaven and earth. Three is the three powers. All of these arise from the nothingness of the principle of the Great Ultimate Void. The ten thousand things begin with the Tao. The Tao is the source of all: surely this is the principle of nature?" If that is so, if you do not attain this in your studies you will not master the subtleties of swordsmanship.'"

The visitor said, "essentially swordsmanship is victory and defeat. For example, if you attain one-ness, you do not heed victory. Discarding victory you achieve complete victory. I can't make head or tail of it."

The master replied, "In the *Laozi* it says, 'The virtuous do not display virtue; therefore they achieve virtue. Those of lesser virtue strive not to lose virtue, therefore they are not virtuous.' When swordsmanship gives up victory, it naturally achieves victory. It is when they cannot give up their attachment to winning that everyone suffers defeat. Giving up victory and emerging victorious is just bringing about the realization of the one principle through losing your ego. Not giving up victory is when you cling to your desires and preserve the sense of yourself.

"Again it says, 'Those of great virtue do nothing, yet nothing is left undone. Those of lesser virtue act, yet there is always something to be done.' If we take swordsmanship, a master has innumerable changes of technique, infinite variety, yet his mind is not limited to any particular form, he is simply in a state of *mushin*. Because he is in *mushin*, it is said he 'does' nothing. The range of inner and outer techniques of the opponent does not affect your mind. It also includes what in Shinto is called the Purification of the Six Roots of Perception. Although we refer to discarding these things in this school, when they are discarded, you do not lack in expertise. It corresponds to 'thus there is nothing that is not done.' The minds of those who are set on winning are full of the possibilities of what they were taught, initiation, and thoughts of Buddhist teaching. With all these things in their minds, when they come to take a position, are absolutely determined not to lose their chance of victory. Whereupon, frozen like statues, colored by the inner and outer possibilities of the enemy's disposition, hesitating and unable to move freely, they are all defeated. When the mind is full, you cannot naturally reach the state of *mushin*, technique and theory will not transform, there will be no connection between myself and the opponent; when there is no connection between things they become separated and thus come into conflict, unable to obtain freedom.

"You should look at human affairs nowadays. Those who utilize gentleness are unopposed; those who have discovered the principle of the way have no enemies under heaven; they are always victorious no matter who they face, living in freedom. Again, those with a strong stubborn nature will be opposed, they will not be without enemies, will always suffer great defeats and will not be free. So, my master once said, 'This is an iron-clad law. What you put out you will get back. Be it for good or evil, however you act, you will reap the consequences thereof.' Furthermore, 'If transformation is nature, then not transforming is the self. Order is natural; disorder is based on the self. Therefore we hear the flexible are able to control the strong. Thus we should strike; thus we should win.'

"In the *Analects of Confucius* it says, 'When Jiangzi asked Confucius about politics, saying 'if we take the argument that killing the wicked will bring about goodness, what is your position on this?' Confucius demurred, 'what need is there to kill in the pursuit of politics? If I desire goodness, the people are already good. The superior man's virtue is the wind. The lesser man's virtue is the grass. The grass will bend if the wind blows upon it.' Thus is it not foolish to say that killing is necessary for victory in swordsmanship? Remote, immovable, when I embody virtue and principle, though it may be said I do not strive for victory, the enemy just falls. Great benevolence has no need to kill. People will be ruined by their own actions."

The visitor said, "I am altogether convinced. So swordsmanship should be as it is in these few schools, the Unchu-ryu, Yagyu-ryu, and the Mugan-ryu. Study in other schools results in learning things that are dangerous."

The master said, "you are mistaken. If you take it as essentially one school, there is no distinction between oneself and others. If you extend the proceeding statement, with reference to one's own school, are not all the others mistaken? If that seems to be so, my judgement is not a public statement. It's just that Yagyu Munenori, Miura Masanari, and so on, in recent times are surpassed in great numbers by those with name and position, but when you look at them, they certainly don't know how to teach so that practice and principle are consistent. If this is so, they can only say they are close to the way. Whatever the school, it embodies the principle. Those who discover it should be thought of as possessing a treasure. They should be valued. Beyond this, wherever you look now, they would be despised and disliked by people who covet nothing but victory. There will be no end to this decline into corruption. Amongst followers of Confucius and Mengzi too, recent times have seen the rise of countless factions, departing from the path of morality, humanity, and justice, which have themselves just become words to be rearranged and played with. As the tip moves increasingly further from the point of origin, as the world of the sages becomes increasingly distant in time, so it comes to be like this. Our swordsmanship seems like this, too. If these people do not perish, they will simply split into innumerable styles, abandoning the virtue of the style, just devising choreographed patterns, which will be all that's left. Is it not tragic?"

The visitor said, "what you have said, master, I can completely understand. If that is so, as I have understood it, learning this art is difficult. Is this so?"

The master said, "traces of the principle are to be found throughout the whole of the written language. This is, in itself, not the correct principle at all. According to these traces, you must understand that which leaves no trace. Is that not why Zen priests say you must understand it intuitively? That's why you must drop from your consciousness all that you have seen or heard, so the mind can unrestrainedly grasp the principle of the way. It is difficult for the mind to become like this, though there are many who have studied and learnt by heart the wisdom of the sutras of the sages. The reason there is no one who has discovered the way is that few people have reached the wisdom of the sages. Although it may come as a shock, it is this serious deficiency of the thinking mind that prevents the light of the spirit from opening."

The visitor said, "leaving aside the thinking mind, detaching ourselves from our crutch, we will not recognize it and take it up just by chance. How can we realize the correct principle?"

The master replied, "simple things are difficult if you are very busy. Therefore, as I explained before, from when you are a novice you are training to bring about the match of principle and practice. Even so, it may be difficult to realise it though you spend your whole life searching. You should not look to other people for the correct principle. As Confucius said, 'The superior man seeks for it in himself; the inferior man seeks for it in others.'"

The visitor said, "if this is so, does that mean the ultimate level in swordsmanship is not passed on?"

The master replied, "the ultimate level is something that the teacher should be sure to teach well. Of course it is something that must have been attained by the teachers themselves. As related above, they can then guide others. As with scholarship, if you haven't attained it yourself, you will not rise to the level of profound subtlety. Ascending to the mysteries yourself is, in the case of swordsmanship, also called 'the waters of the West River,' 'sword striking the arrow,' and 'mu ichi tou' (not one sword). Though this may be so, teachers and their students should continue to pass this down permanently. When choreographed set patterns are all that's left behind, those in the west will seek the principal in the east. In the present day, attitudes such as he is of a house of swordsmanship, this is a spear school, seem to proliferate. Virtue is not something which is transmitted through the generations. It is of this person, not of this house."

The visitor asked, "just what are the profound mysteries?"

The master replied, "they are unknowable."

The guest asked, "so, is that not ignorance?"

The master replied, "it is not. They can be known, and yet not understood."

The visitor asked, "how can this be so?"

The master replied, "though it is like knowing, it is not knowing. All I can say is they are beyond understanding."

Acknowledgments

My own understanding of swordsmanship is the result of many years of training under the expert tuition of Ryu Seigo and his son, Ryu Seiki. For this, and much else, I am deeply grateful.

It goes without saying that any inaccuracies in interpretation are entirely my own.